**LIVES &
LEGACIES**

Pope John XXIII

SERIES EDITOR: BARBARA LEAH ELLIS

CHRISTIAN FELDMAN

Pope John XXIII

A Spiritual Biography

Translated by Peter Heinegg

A Crossroad 8th Avenue Book
The Crossroad Publishing Company
New York

The Crossroad Publishing Company
481 Eighth Avenue, New York, NY 10001

First published in German in 2000 by Verlag Herder Freiburg im Breisgau
First published in English in 2000 by The Crossroad Publishing Company

LIBRARY OF CONGRESS CATALOGING-IN-PUBLICATION DATA
Feldman, Christian.
Pope John XXIII: a spiritual biography / Christian Feldman.
    p. cm.
Includes bibliographical references and index.
ISBN 0-8245-2356-3
1. John XXIII, Pope, 1881-1963. I. Title.
    BX1378.2 .F37   2000
        282'.092—dc21
        00-010192 CIP

Printed in the United States of America
Set in Janson
Designed and produced by SCRIBES Editorial
Cover design by Kaeser and Wilson Design Ltd.

1 2 3 4 5 6 7 8 9 10 04 03 02 01 00

CONTENTS

Pope John XXIII

Roncalli as the bishop's secretary in Bergamo, 1919.
Courtesy Helmuth Nils Loose/Alpha Omega, Levallois-Perret

Prologue

"*UN GRASSO!* A FATTY!" the distinguished lady on St. Peter's Square exclaimed in horror, dropped her binoculars and seemed about to faint. The newly elected pope had appeared on the loggia of St. Peter's—on foot, without the customary splendid sedan chair, a squat figure with the face of a good-humored peasant. It was October 28, 1958. As Angelo Roncalli himself was well aware, he was not especially photogenic: "Oh God," he sighed, a few days after the election, as he observed his emphatic nose and his huge protruding ears in a mirror, "What a disaster this fellow will be on TV!"

The contrast to his predecessor couldn't have been greater: Pius XII had ruled the Catholic Church for two decades like an absolute monarch; and he looked like an archangel. Everything about him seemed otherworldly: the tall, thin figure; the chiseled profile; the eyes, beneath his shining rimless glasses, often gazing off into the distance; the majestic gestures; the style, at once incantatory and muscle-flexing, of his speeches. He solemnly read his messages from the printed text before him, every one of them polished down to the last word, like a mini-encyclopedia.

When he made his appearances, one could sense something of a heavenly glow. But even when he ecstatically stretched out his arms and proclaimed his concern for the victims of war and bombings, and begged God for peace, he struck people as remarkably alien and distant. When he gave the papal blessing, his skinny hands sliced through the air like knives. Catholics saw in him something like a king. Some of them groaned beneath his regime, others revered him as an ambassador from the heavenly hosts; few people actually loved him.

And now this cheerful conversationalist, who couldn't hide his peasant roots even after fifty years as a clerical diplomat and bishop! He didn't walk, he waddled. As the cameras rolled, he scratched behind his ears and blew his nose at the microphone. He loved to make impromptu speeches, where he got carried away and held forth endlessly. At official receptions in the modest residence of the Patriarch of Venice, he told jokes and served up delicious anecdotes. He was no monarch, but a grandpa. He had no starry-eyed majesty, but lots of earthiness and familiar intimacy. The writer Marie Luise Kaschnitz was moved to call him a "human being disguised as pope." At the time of his election the Catholic world was rather disappointed.

Where did he come from, this seventy-seven-year-old surprise-pope? Pius was an authentic Roman, from a noble family of jurists; his father had served the Vatican as a lawyer. The Roncallis, by contrast, had been planting corn and wheat for centuries in the fields of a little village in Lombardy called Sotto il Monte—unheard of!

As a schoolboy—eager reporters soon announced—Angelo Roncalli may have stolen pumpkins, but the report cards he brought home were nothing special. He had neither a pastor's experience in caring for souls nor a curialist's experience with the church bureaucracy.

On the contrary, in his youth church authorities had suspected him of "modernism." Just to keep him out of trouble the Vatican had sent him off to the Balkans to the most trivial and isolated diplomatic posts. At sixty-three he was finally given the honorable assignment of papal nuncio to Paris; at seventy-one he was made cardinal and patriarch of the important diocese of Venice. Fair enough, a sort of late bloomer—but pope?

The word was, he had been a compromise candidate. At the conclave archconservatives and progressives had blocked each other; and so the seventy-seven-year-old was elected, a *papa di passaggio*, the newspapers wrote somewhat scornfully, a transitional pope. How right they were. The Cardinal of Brussels, Leon Suenens, a pioneer of the conciliar reform movement, put it this way: "From the perspective of history we can undoubtedly say that he opened a new age for the Church, that he laid out the boundary posts for the transition from the twentieth to the twenty-first century."

In fact the stopgap candidate of 1958 unleashed a landslide in the Catholic Church. In the mere four and a half years of his papacy the Catholic Church acquired a more human and inviting face. It opened its doors wide to the questions and crises of the men and women "out there." For centuries this Church had looked like a great block of stone, immovable, in repose, encapsulated in a mixture of complacency and fear.

Pope Roncalli had a completely different approach to life. "The world is moving," he once noted. "We have to find the right access to it, with a youthful and confident heart, and not waste time on confrontation. I prefer keeping stride with someone who's walking, instead of going off by myself and letting people pass me by."

Mistrustfully walling himself off was not his style. He showed that he was capable of learning, curious, enthusiastic for dialogue. He was completely different from the self-righteous fundamentalists who think they already know everything down to the last detail. His powerful, simple peasant faith wasn't afraid of rubbing shoulders; he never vetoed discussion; and so he managed to challenge seemingly self-evident things and to leave the beaten track far behind.

During one audience Pope John confided to his listeners what he wanted from the Church: "It's important to always keep moving and not to rest on traditional paths. We have to keep seeking new contacts, and to always be receptive for the legitimate challenges of the time in which we are called to live, so that Christ may be proclaimed and recognized in every way."

This from a man about to complete the eighth decade of his life.

The courtyard of the simple peasant house in Lombardy, where Angelo Giuseppe Roncalli was born in November 25, 1881. *Courtesy* Herder, Rome

1

Fields and Vineyards

Poor, but as a child born of reverent and modest people,
I am especially glad to die poor.

—*Angelo Giuseppe Roncalli*

IN THE LATE AFTERNOON of November 25, 1881, the *tramontana*, the icy northern Italian wind, was blowing from the mountains; and it was pouring rain as the peasant woman Marianna Roncalli, twenty-seven years old, warmly wrapped her fourth child (born that morning) and took him down to the rectory of Sotto il Monte to be baptized. Don Francesco Rebuzzini, the village pastor, was off in Bergamo just then or perhaps in a neighboring village visiting the sick—we're not sure.

Marianna, her husband Giovanni, great-uncle Zaverio as godfather and, of course tiny Angelino, as he would thenceforth be called, waited patiently on a hard bench. Giovanni—a mustachioed, dark-haired man with kind, sharp eyes, whose photos call to mind the classic Roncalli nose and the future pope's protruding ears—was smiling in quiet satisfaction. After three daughters he finally had a son, a boy to take care of the fields and vineyards when he was too old to work.

Don Rebuzzini was back now, and the little group walked to the nearby church of Santa Maria Assunta, the Assumption, where Maria had married Giovanni. Today was yet another joyful occasion: The youngest Roncalli was being received into the community of the faithful.

Thus began the simple, straightforward life of Angelo Giuseppe

Roncalli. Sotto il Monte, literally "Under the Mountain," was a village, or rather a collection of scattered farmsteads near Bergamo, where the Po valley meets the foothills of the Alps. At any rate, it had twelve hundred inhabitants and plain, slate-covered stone houses with red brick floors. In the summer it smelled of clover and wheat, on the slopes grew modest vines (*ronchi*, the word for vineyard terraces, whence perhaps the name Roncalli), and over the lazily flowing Adda river there usually hung a breath of mist.

The house of Angelo's parents was by no means as wretched as people like to imagine. More than three hundred years old, and quite spacious, it had three stories and two courtyards. To be sure, things were very cramped in the interconnected rooms, because the Roncallis were an extended family with sometimes as many as thirty-four members. They had around ten acres of land and six cows.

Giovanni Roncalli was a *mezzadro*, a sharecropper—-more than a day laborer, less than a farmer. The land belonged to a rich man from Bergamo who provided the capital while Giovanni did the work; and the yield was split between them. The Roncallis planted corn, cabbage, and wheat, pressed a strong, slightly sour wine, and raised silk worms. The soil was hard and stony; meals consisted of soup and polenta; there was seldom any meat, and a piece of cake only at Christmas and Easter. Still there was always a place in the kitchen and a warm dinner for a beggar. As Roncalli later recalled in Rome, "We were very poor, but everyone was poor, and we didn't notice that we lacked anything."

Angelo and his twelve brothers and sisters grew up in a believing but in no way hyper-religious atmosphere. Peasants in Lombardy have no time for outlandish pious exercises. The first pilgrimage of Angelo's life led him exactly one kilometer from Sotto il Monte to the shrine of the *Madonna delle Canever*, Our Lady of the Winepresses. His mother, who was pregnant again, took her two smallest children, cradled in her arms. Angelo, who was four years old at the time, and three of his siblings, trotted alongside. By the time they had climbed the steep mountain path to the chapel, mass was already underway and the little church was packed with people.

As an old man of eighty, Pope John once told a group of pilgrims, in a gently melancholic tone, how his mother lifted up the children, one after another, to the window railing and let them look in. "My mother lifted me up and said: 'Look, Angelo, how beautiful the Madonna is. I have dedicated you completely to her.' This is the first clear memory that I have of my childhood."

But he was far from glorifying his early years and the harsh everyday life of the *mezzadri*. As pope he once laconically remarked that there were "three ways for a man to do himself in: women, gambling, and farming. My father chose the most boring way." His father, he said, "was simple and good, a peasant who slaved away all day long with digging, hoeing, and so forth." Little Angelo helped him as best he could with the grape harvest and did his part caring for the livestock. He laid out turnip cuttings and dragged manure out onto the fields.

Family life in the Roncalli house hardly seems to have been idyllic. "In our house," the twenty-six-year-old Angelo wrote to his sister Ancilla from Bergamo, "the evil habit prevails of making nasty faces and frequently growling for no reason at all. You mustn't do things that way . . ." And as late as 1948, in his Christmas letter to his brother Giovanni, the man who had been promoted to papal nuncio in Paris felt a shudder when he wrote: "Fortunately, my brothers, you don't imitate our old grandfather and great-uncle, who never spoke to one another except when they were quarreling . . . I recall that when I was a small boy I used to fervently beg the Lord in church to make the old Roncallis talk to each other a little."

Fortunately, there was another great-uncle, Zaverio, the *barba* or beard, as old bachelors were called in the country around Bergamo. He set the tone in the family councils, and brought a bit of the outside world to Sotto il Monte. *Zio barba* subscribed to several newspapers; he was one of the founding members of the socially committed "Catholic Action" in Bergamo, and knew all sorts of things about missionary countries. Zaverio must have opened little Angelo's eyes to the fact that faith meant more than rosary beads and Christmas crèches.

Every day Angelo walked four miles back and forth to school through the hill country—barefoot, to spare his expensive leather shoes. Angelo liked attending school, to the amazement of some of his comrades, including his brother Zaverio, who went to school only when it was raining. "That's how it happened," Zaverio recalled, "that he became pope and I remained illiterate."

This educational institution consisted of a single room with three benches, one for each age group. Angelo seems to have been a thoroughly normal pupil, with no special achievements to his record. None, that is, until he caused a minor sensation during the visit of the government school inspector, who asked the children of Sotto il Monte the old trick question: "What's heavier, a hundred pounds of straw or a hundred pounds of iron?" "A hundred pounds of iron!" the swarm of children shouted, except for Angelo who coolly maintained that a hundred pounds was a hundred pounds.

In later years the pope's erstwhile classmates naturally informed his biographers that even back then they could tell Angelo would amount to something. "Roncalli got everything in a flash," said Battistel, who had been an ironmonger in Sotto il Monte. Angelo's brother Giuseppe stressed the boy's phenomenal memory: "Even now, where he's pope, in the middle of a church full of people he can recognize a face that he saw one time when as a young priest. He was that way ever since he was little." That may be right, but we also know that Pope John had a hard time remembering names.

Don Rebuzzini, the country priest with heart and soul, who knew about every sick calf and every greenfly-infestation in his parish, but who was also educated and well read, stood up to *Zio barba* on Angelo's behalf: Was this bright young lad really going to be nothing more than a sharecropper? Obviously Angelo had dreamt out loud about being a priest; at least he had told his cousin Camilla about it, a girl with whom he liked to play and go off on adventures. Once they crept into a house where a wake was being held, so they could see a corpse. They found the dead old woman in a musty dark room, her mouth wide open and a creepy expression on her face. They ran away in terror.

Only now did Don Rebuzzini and great-uncle Zaverio get Angelo Latin lessons with Pietro Bolis, the pastor in the neighboring village of Carvico, and Italian lessons with his curate. Both achieved only limited results—surely due to the fact that while Don Bolis was generous with beatings, he didn't have much pedagogical talent to spare. "I had to translate and find the nominatives and accusatives," Roncalli later reported concerning his lessons on Caesar, "and if I made a mistake, he hit me. Sometimes he made me kneel outside in the street."

Even when he was pope, Bolis's unfortunate pupil had to practice his conversational Latin in preparation for the Council, and his Italian always had a clear dialectical flavor. At audiences with groups of pilgrims from the old home he delighted to speak Bergamask.

After a year Angelo was allowed to exchange the corporal punishment from his language teacher for an episcopal theological college—a minor seminary—in Celana. Even though, apart from a little Latin, he had barely mastered any of the high school subjects, at nine years of age he was put into the third form, where he sat side by side with thirteen- and fourteen-year-olds. These pupils, most of whom came from bourgeois families, mocked their undersized classmate for his peasant manners; and the Latin teacher was an even more brutal slave-driver than Don Bolis. As Angelo said, "He managed to make me forget the little Latin I knew." He brought home similarly bad grades in Italian and math.

In addition, he didn't feel good at all with the relatives in whose house he had been lodged. Perhaps he also had guilt-feelings toward his father, who was unhappy about having to do without Angelo's powerful hands: "He's the son of a poor peasant," Giovanni grumbled, "and he'll be a poor priest."

Finally a saving angel entered the picture in the form of Don Rebuzzini. For a whole summer he crammed Angelo for the minor seminary in Bergamo, and did it so tactfully that the boy took pleasure in learning and developed a real sense of himself. Soon afterwards Don Rebuzzini introduced him to a well-born cleric from Bergamo, Count Borlani. The count's brother owned the land that the Roncallis tilled. Angelo made such a good impression on Borlani that he offered to pay for his education all the way to ordination. The way had been paved, and his father Giovanni heaved a sigh of relief.

But Angelo, who always got by on very little and, as a Vatican diplomat, always put something aside for his unmarried sisters, impoverished seminarians, and an orphanage, would never forget his simple roots. When he was nuncio in Paris, as he told his brother Zaverio, he once went to a reception in the feudal Elysée Palace when suddenly he thought of his mother: "It was as if mother had popped out of a corner and, in her stunned simplicity, said, 'Madonna! How in the world did my Giovanni wind up here?'"

His mother! She didn't want to send off her boy on the trip to Bergamo without a penny. For a whole day she ran from one neighbor to another, and collected a total of two lire, about twenty-five cents in today's money. A ridiculous sum, which she laid on the table before Angelo that evening, in tears.

Bergamo: the city of Gaetano Donizetti and the commedia dell'arte, stamped by the Renaissance, a small town, but not a sleepy burg.

Bergamo, where working conditions in the factories were so wretched, was considered the center of social Catholicism in Italy. The people of Bergamo were fiercely loyal to the pope and produced more candidates for the priesthood then any other diocese in the country; but they were also intellectually nimble, with political minds of their own, and burningly interested in new ideas.

To be sure, this new spirit had yet to reach the boys' boarding school where Roncalli was enrolled from 1892 to 1895, or the seminary where he spent another five years. There they continued to offer a (thoroughly loving and joyful) ghetto education in the old style. There he was protected from the temptations of a godless world, shielded from competing models of life (newspapers were forbidden, even *L'Osservatore Romano*). There they had painfully exact self-control, a daily schedule regulated down to the minute, with worship and study, private devotion and examination of conscience, preaching, "the great silence" and spiritual reading at table.

Angelo developed a fiery zeal for smoothing out the rough edges and individual features of his personality and eradicating every conceivable forbidden pleasure. The strict house rules of the seminary weren't enough for him. When he was only fourteen years old, he received permission to follow the stringent *Little Rules*, which were reserved for especially assiduous candidates. Angelo copied them out carefully into a notebook. They now make up the first pages of his famous *Diary of the Soul*, which he kept from then on until the end of his life, with detailed resolutions, terrible self-criticism when he failed to keep them, and brooding conversations with God. After his death the pope's diary became a bestseller, but most readers probably laid it aside after a few pages. Nowadays the piety it contains seems too tame and drab, its daily agenda too mechanical ("Between 6 and 9 p.m. pray five 'Our Fathers' and 'Hail Marys' in honor of the five wounds of Our Lord Jesus Christ and perform at least three acts of self-denial in honor of the Mother of God").

"Up until now I have always played with God, but one doesn't play with God," the youth notes fearfully, and vows to avoid "idle comrades." Obviously even in the Bergamo seminary there were worldly lads "who like to have dealings with persons of the opposite sex and talk about love stories, who often visit guest houses and are immoderate, particularly in drinking; who want to get a reputation for being vengeful, contentious, and unscrupulous." When people were playing cards or shooting craps, he didn't "even want to look." He forbade himself to engage in roughhousing with friends and casting casual glances at women: "You should avoid even the slightest intimacy with them that could be in any way dangerous or suspicious."

One has to grant the young seminarian this much: for the most part he hadn't made up this program himself, with all its fear of life and piously veiled contempt for the world. By the end of his period of formation, when he became a prefect and had to keep an eye on his younger comrades, he revealed a much more open attitude; his piety had become more human. One of his fellow seminarians used to go around all day with his eyes lowered and would never make eye contact with the others. Roncalli called him aside and explained to him, as he later writes, "that it was tyranny to live this way, and that he should avoid exaggeration in anything except the love of God." The shy seminarian did get ordained, but later left the priesthood.

Meanwhile Roncalli was enjoying his studies; he began to take an interest in history, and rummaged through Bergamo's glorious past. He wasn't bothered by the fact that in the seminary he was getting only a narrow-gauge philosophical and theological education. It was solid, but had no great intellectual pretensions. Did he ever dream of going to a university, perhaps even a secular one? We don't know.

Instead, he was having problems breaking away from his family. When he returned to Sotto Il Monte for the summer vacation, some of his relatives made it clear that they considered him an arrogant little upstart who just wanted to make a comfortable life for himself with his seminary studies. Did he have to constantly grind away at his textbooks while his brothers and sisters slaved away in the fields? Sometimes someone would complain (as Angelo himself commented to his mother) that Mamma Roncalli was serving her eldest son better food than the others got. For her part, his mother was hurt by thoughtless remarks from her son. Angelo writes in his diary: "In the course of it I had something to say about her curiosity. She was very offended . . . And if she was sad on my account, I was even sadder when I saw her sadness and, to speak frankly, her weakness."

Angelo's letters from the seminary that he entered in 1901 sound all the more amiable—but also a bit relieved to have escaped the ongoing domestic conflict. The twenty-year-old got a scholarship to the Pontificio Seminario San Apollinare, which had an outstanding reputation, and was a real scholarly institution. A theological college specially intended for gifted students from the Bergamo region, financed by a foundation that dated from the seventeenth century, it forms part of the papal seminary. The building today looks gray and gloomy. Angelo's room reminds one of a prison cell: the bed as hard as a plank, a single, grilled window high up near the ceiling. But the village lad who had been promoted to a Roman was full of enthusiasm. "We live like princes," he wrote home and raved about the good food.

2

Roman Splendor, the
"Barbarous" Military and
the Strikers

*He who is deaf, blind and silent
lives a hundred years in peace.*
—*Sicilian proverb*

EVERY MORNING HE COMMENDED his loved ones to the Madonna in
the house chapel. There was so much to see in the Eternal City! At
an academic conference in the seminary of the Propaganda Fide he
heard future missionaries deliver reports about their studies in forty
languages. "All the colors were there, white, yellow, red. Some of
them had faces and hands as black as coal. And the pope? I managed
to see him on Sunday evening in St. Peter's amid thousands of
lights. I was able to get close to him . . . And he, that good old man,
sends his blessing to all of you. . . . Addio! May the Lord bless you!
Your cleric, Angelo."

The "kindly old man" in the Vatican was Leo XIII. He was then
almost ninety years old; he had been reigning for twenty-two years,
but still showed astonishing intellectual agility. He greeted the
opening of the twentieth century with an enthusiastic hymn —in
Latin, of course. Leo is often considered the first "modern" pope.
He venerated Galileo, once condemned by the magisterium; he
founded the Vatican observatory; he inaugurated a college for literature and literary criticism. He also opened the Vatican archives to
researchers and liked to quote Cicero's demand: "The first rule for
the historian is to tell the truth, and then not to conceal anything
that is true." Broadly educated, open to the world, a critical ques-

The barely twenty-two-year-old Angelo
Roncalli in 1901 as a soldier of the Seventy-
third Infantry Regiment in Bergamo.
Courtesy Helmut Niles Loose/Alpha Omega,
Leveallois-Perret

tioner, he tried to involve the Church in a dialogue with contemporary culture. Instead of talking about "schismatics" and "heretics," he preferred to call them "separated brothers," and he challenged Catholics to work together with "all decent people."

When Roncalli was himself elected pope almost sixty years later, he continued this uninhibited style, although he had only seen the end of Leo's reign. After a few months he was forced to leave the Pontificio Seminario again. The one-time peasant boy had just won a prize for his performance in a Hebrew examination, when he was called up to do his military service—a "barbarous" duty for clerics, he thought. As recruit no. 11331-42 he entered the Bergamo barracks to spend the next year as a member of the 73rd infantry regiment of the Lombardy Brigade.

Although he didn't like the service at all and called it his "Babylonian captivity," his superiors were satisfied with Private Roncalli. They gave him good marks in rifle training, promoted him to corporal and later to sergeant. He once was put under arrest because some of his men were guilty of some sort of insubordination.

He had a far worse time with the sleazy barracks atmosphere, with the crude sexual boasting and fantasies of his comrades, who tried to cope with their hormones by bragging in the grand style. Roncalli was confused, outraged, shocked. "How ugly the world is, how repellent, how dirty," he noted in his diary. "The military is a wellspring that surges up from putrefaction and overflows the cities. . . . I never thought that rational people could debase themselves like this." Breathing a sigh of relief he returned to Rome, where altogether different temptations awaited him. These were more intellectual and hid behind book covers and in conversations with friends. "I have a vehement longing to know everything," Angelo noted, "to become acquainted with every important author, to keep abreast of every scholarly current in all their many directions."

A laudable undertaking for a student, one might think. But the winds on the Tiber shifted when in 1903 Pope Leo XIII died and the patriarch of Venice, Giuseppe Sarto, was chosen to succeed him. Pius X, as he called himself, was a charming pastor and a simple soul, full of anxiety about uncontrolled thoughts and the free play of the mind.

In his decrees and encyclicals the pope condemned everything he thought un-Catholic or whatever—as some of the kinder church historians nowadays make allowances for him—he couldn't understand. His insinuating advisers came up with a cruelly perfected system of denunciation and a spectral concept that threatened to brand as heretical any deviation from religious business as usual: *modernism.*

Roncalli loved and revered the new pope, who, like him, was the son of a northern Italian peasant. But he thought and acted differently—instinctively and impartially, without being aware of it. In his diary he promised to strive for "harmony, balance, and clarity of judgment."

> On controversial points I will, as an ignorant person, rather be silent than make bold assertions that deviate in even the slightest way from the doctrinal sense of the Church."

In the same breath, however, he adds to the palette of his resolutions an "intelligent and circumspect breadth of views" and defends his love of critical thinking:

> I keep up with new lines of thought, with their incessant development, and study the various trends. For me criticism is light, and truth is holy and indivisible.

Leo XIII had put it just the same way. Undeterred, young seminarian Roncalli cultivated dangerous friendships, with people like Ernesto Buonaiuti, an extremely bright professor of church history at Rome's Sapienza University who was excommunicated in 1924 and driven from his position in 1934 at the behest of Mussolini's Black Shirts. Roncalli had been assigned Buonaiuti by lot as his companion for his walks through Rome. He couldn't do anything about that, because it was the custom in the seminary; but then he sought out Buonaiuti, who was only a little older than himself, and newly ordained, to assist at his own ordination.

As pope he would still openly admit that he learned a lot from the excommunicated man. He respectfully called him by his priestly title, "Don Ernesto," and dedicated a "sad memory" to him in an entry in his diary that cannot be dated precisely. On Good Saturday, 1946 Buonaiuti had died, full of warm love for the Church that had outlawed him. Roncalli remarks: "Of course, there was no priest on hand to bless his body, and no church to offer him a place of burial . . . Words from his spiritual testament [Buonaiuti's] . . . 'I may have erred, but when I look at the essentials of what I have taught, I find nothing to renounce or recant.' *Dominus parcat illi* (May the Lord spare him)." At the Roman diocesan synod Pope John had a resolution passed that unfortunate and excommunicated priests were not to be abandoned, but kept in touch with.

Italy's former prime minister, Giulio Andreotti, who liked to talk openly and proudly about his relationships with popes and curial prelates, once alluded to Roncalli's friendship with Don Giulio Belvederi. According to Andreotti, Belvederi was a capable biblical scholar who never got a university chair because of his preference for texts damned as "modernist." On the evening after his election as pope, "around 10 o'clock" Andreotti claims John XXIII called up his old friend Belvederi in Rome's Priscilla theological college, where he was spending his retirement, and chatted with him for twenty minutes.

In July 1904 the twenty-two-year-old Roncalli received his doctorate in theology. The assistant at the written exam was Monsignore Eugenio Pacelli, later Pius XII, who was already active in the Vatican Secretariat of State. On August 10, Angelo Giuseppe Roncalli was ordained in the somewhat obscure church of Santa Maria in Monte Santo on Rome's Piazza del Popolo. His parents and great-uncle Zaverio couldn't be there because the train fare cost too much, but they were delighted to come to Angelo's first mass at home in Sotto il Monte five days later on the feast of the Assumption.

Roncalli's very first mass had taken place in Rome, in the crypt of St. Peter's, where he would be buried sixty years later. This was followed by an audience with Pope Pius X, who had only been in office for one year and who liked to do this favor for new priests. When Angelo knelt before him, he affably asked him when he would be back home. "On the Assumption," Angelo stammered excitedly. Whereupon the pope, smiling dreamily, said: "What a feast that will be, up in the little village, and in that beautiful Bergamo countryside, and how festively the bells will ring out!"

Back in Rome, Roncalli began special studies in canon law, gave a few ill-fated lectures to pious associations ("a fiasco") and watched in bewilderment at the rapid march of changes in the Church's government. One of the most prominent victims of these changes was Monsignore Giacomo Maria Radini-Tedeschi, who after a few months became Roncalli's employer—and beyond that his model, father figure, and destiny.

Radini-Tedeschi was an elegant, stately figure, from a noble family of German-Swiss extraction that had always been socially committed. In 1890 his father organized counseling centers in major Italian cities to defend the artisans organizations against a recent law seizing their assets for purposes favored by the state. The son continued this family tradition. Angular, irascible, authoritarian, but with a heart of gold, he fought for the rights of the Church of the little people, not with "pinpricks" but with "cannons," as Roncalli later put it.

At thirty-three, with his degrees in theology and canon law, Radini-Tedeschi was called to the Secretariat of State and entrusted with important missions in Vienna and Paris. He felt free to turn down Pope Leo's offer to dedicate himself entirely to the diplomatic service and make a career as a nuncio. As he supposedly replied to a disappointed Holy Father, the refinements of diplomacy ran contrary to his Christian conscience.

Instead, he was now allowed to coordinate the activities of the Catholic associations of Italy, to travel around as a speaker—in the Holy Year of 1900 alone he had 1,300 engagements—and function as a spiritual director of the *Opera dei Congressi*, the social organizations of Italian Catholicism. The movement had naturally started out from Bergamo and within a short time comprised, in that diocese alone, around 200 consumer groups, insurance and housing cooperatives, credit banks for peasants and unskilled laborers, winegrowers associations, cooperative mills, soup kitchens, etc.

The Catholics involved in all this—there were at least 40,000 of them in the diocese of Bergamo—could consider themselves loyal followers of Pope Leo XIII. In his pregnant 1891 encyclical *Rerum novarum* Leo had reckoned social renewal as one of the Church's key tasks. He argued that neither Christian charities nor the laws of the state alone could heal an unjust situation where production and commerce threatened to degenerate into a "monopoly of the few" and where "a handful of all-powerful rich persons imposed what amounted to the yoke of slavery on the propertyless masses." The fruits of labor belonged to those who did the labor. The pope sought to chart an independent path for Christian justice between socialism and liberalism. He thought it important that the people affected by injustice should organize to solve their problems; and so he strengthened the Catholic labor movement.

Of course, when Catholics became involved in the "social question," they fell afoul of another Vatican guideline, which urged them to stay out of politics altogether. Ever since the downfall of the Papal States the popes had felt themselves the victims of the Italian unification movement. In the new nation of Italy Catholics were not supposed to feel at home. However, more and more lay people wanted the pope to break loose from the old days, to look upon the loss of his secular power as liberation, and regain a place for Catholicism in the political life of Italy. These currents later gave rise to the *Democrazia cristiana*, the Christian Democratic party.

Here, too, Bergamo led the way. Granted, the great majority of Catholics obediently sat out the parliamentary elections. But they voted so unanimously in the local elections that they took over almost the entire administration. Catholic convictions were not some old museum piece, said Professor Niccolò Rezzara, leader of the social movement in Bergamo. The only way to stop socialism and anarchy was to put an end to one's own laziness.

The new pope could not have been pleased to see lay people relying—successfully—on their own judgment. The social movement, he admitted, did not promote such horrendous errors as modernism, but it was more attractive and therefore all the more dangerous. Pius X brought all these activities to a halt. Without further ado he dissolved the *Opera dei Congressi* and he used the old method of kicking people upstairs to remove Monsignore Radini-Tedeschi from the

Vatican's power center: he appointed him bishop of Bergamo.

Perhaps it wasn't a punitive transfer, as people thought at the time; because, as the focal point of social Catholicism, the diocese was, so to speak, tailor-made for the new bishop. Catholic social and relief organizations continued to function in Bergamo thanks to a special papal authorization. And, in a highly unusual move, Pius personally consecrated Radini-Tedeschi as bishop. One of the ministers at the service was Angelo Roncalli.

Radini-Tedeschi, an aristocrat from Piacenza, asked the rector of the San Apollinare seminary to get him a secretary who knew the mentality and problems of Bergamo. A number of young priests were tested by having them handle the bishop's correspondence. Finally, the forty-seven-year-old Radini-Tedeschi picked Roncalli, now twenty-three. He was the "most thoroughly Roman," it was said; and Angelo took that for high praise.

From then on he was considered the "shadow" of his bishop. Anyone who wanted to see Radini-Tedeschi had to get over the hurdle of Roncalli. He knew everything, prepared all the appointments, was present at delicate discussions, always alert and observant—and yet discreet, silent, and reserved to the point of self-denial. These qualities left a decisive stamp on the Roncalli who would later be a diplomat and church leader.

Over the next four years the new bishop visited a total of 352 parishes in his diocese. He saw to the renovation of decrepit churches, refurnished the cathedral and installed running water and central heating in the seminary. His secretary participated in all this, and in the process he learned more about modern pastoral care and the very down-to-earth problems accompanying it than he could have gotten from any seminary advisor.

Alongside his bishop, who was brimming with vitality and committed and respected far beyond Bergamo, the former peasant boy came to know "the world" and made a few important contacts: Achille Ratti, director of the Ambrosian Library in Milan and the future Pope Pius XI, who had been a classmate of Radini; and Giacomo della Chiesa, archbishop of Bologna, who was elected

In the First World War Angelo Roncalli served as a non-commissioned medical orderly in northern Italian military hospitals (here in Bergamo, 1915).

pope as Benedict XV in 1914, and who was one of his best friends. The leading personalities of the Catholic social movement were frequent visitors to the episcopal residence of Bergamo; and Roncalli also witnessed the brutal persecution of Cardinal Andrea Carlo Ferrari of Milan, who tried to put the Church back in touch with the world of contemporary culture and the working class.

And naturally he shared the impetuous social passion of his bishop. He helped him set up an office for would-be emigrants, a League of Working Women, and a relief organization for pregnant women, with the poetic name of the *Casa di Maternità*. The bishop's secretary knew the haunts of the union members and the badly heated apartments in the suburban slums.

"Our outstanding Don Roncalli has even tried to organize the women switchboard operators," some people muttered furiously in Bergamo. "If he'd just be satisfied with a union for sextons!"

Sharply worded letters of complaint were sent off to Rome about the bishop and his "shadow," who had aroused the suspicion of the bourgeoisie. This happened when the steelworkers in nearby Ranica went on strike for a shorter workweek—ten and a half hours a day for six days—and slightly higher wages. Of course, their pay was suspended and the threat of being fired constantly hovered over them. The bishop and his secretary were among the few people who organized soup kitchens and subsidies. The Church was sending a mixed message: While the episcopal newspaper of Bergamo set up a fund for the strikers, the right-wing journal *Perseveranza* thundered: "The alms of the bishop are consecrating the strike, a blessing on an openly socialistic cause!"

Roncalli countered with intelligent articles in the church newspaper *La vita dioecesana*: he invoked Pope Leo's case for the unions, and said it was not just the Church's right, but her duty, to get involved in politics. "The priest, who lives in the light of the teachings of the Gospel, can't cross the street and walk on by," he wrote, in an obvious allusion to the priest and levite from the parable of the Good Samaritan, who make their way to Jericho, ignoring the man plundered by robbers and lying in the road. Because Christ had a special love for the disenfranchised, the weak, and the oppressed, "bishops and pastors had the duty to "suffer for the cause of justice."

Pope Pius X, who evidently wasn't always as simplistic in his thinking as some suppose, refused to call the "rabble-rousers" on the carpet: "We cannot chide you for what you have thought prudent to do," he wrote to Bergamo, "since you are the best-informed when it comes to the place, the persons in question and the circumstances." Radini-Tedeschi commented somewhat ironically that some people thought being prudent meant doing nothing. No, "Prudence means acting—and doing the right thing!"

All his life he kept a diary, with simple resolutions and regular examinations of conscience—manuscript entries by Pope John. *Courtesy* Loris Capovilla, "L'ite missa est di papa Giovanni"

3

Roman Spies and Modernism

Angelo Roncalli, suspected of modernism.
—*Ernesto Buonaiuti*

PERHAPS RADINI-TEDESCHI'S REMARK about prudence was also
intended as a mild reproach to his secretary, who had launched into
a wide range of journalistic activities and in so doing didn't always
express himself too diplomatically. While on pilgrimage in the Holy
Land, Roncalli sent the good Catholic newspaper *l'Eco di Bergamo*
sarcastic reports about the horrendous state of the roads: "We
Italians would take something like this for no more than a village
path. . . . But one lives here among the Turks, and the Turkish government is best suited for engaging in extortion and unimaginable
injustices; it has no idea how to build roads." Whenever *La vita
dioecesana* printed an article about some historical subject without a
byline—and there were many such contributions—one could be
pretty sure that it came from the pen of Don Roncalli.

Angelo didn't learn to write more carefully until the modernism
frenzy, whipped up by members of the Roman curia, stretched out
its tentacles after him. On September 1, 1907 the papal encyclical
Pascendi dominici gregis appeared, a shrill declaration of war on the
historical-critical method in theology, on all conceivable demands
for reform within the Church, on the call for sharing power, and
especially on "Americanism," whatever that was. Anyone who
favored or made excuses for "modernism"; anyone who defended

"modernist" theses in history, archeology, or scripture studies; anyone who dared to criticize the Church's magisterium or refused obedience to church authority, would be "forthwith" removed from his church office or professorship.

In Bergamo Rome's hard line led to a conflict when the archconservative Jesuit theologian Guido Matiussi began to stir up trouble in his lectures decrying a whole host of university teachers. He branded the German philosopher Immanuel Kant an enemy of the faith and in a grand, sweeping blow he even came down on Pope Leo XIII. Bishop Radini-Tedeschi ordered his secretary to investigate; Roncalli concluded that the guest speaker had "passed judgment too absolutely and one-sidedly." The truth had to be clearly expressed, "but I couldn't understand why the lectures had to be accompanied by lightning and thunderbolts from Mount Sinai, instead of the serenity and cheerfulness of Jesus by the sea or on the mountain."

In Rome, where there was a smoothly functioning espionage system, the distance that Radini-Tedeschi put between himself and the visiting instigator was no more a secret than Roncalli's private opinions. Pius X personally aired his displeasure with the bishop's failure to toe the line and accused the clergy of Bergamo of preferring unreliable authors. The powerful curial Cardinal De Lai had a word with Roncalli: he had been informed that the bishop's secretary favored a school of thought "that tends to flatly deny the value of tradition and the authority of the past, a dangerous tendency that leads to bad conclusions."

Angelo Roncalli panicked. He wrote De Lai a pious letter and insisted under oath, "that I have never read even a single modernist book, pamphlet or periodical." He boldly concealed the fact that just before this he had published a piece in the church newspaper of Bergamo joining the controversy about a church historian whose work would soon be landing on the Index. He didn't want to take sides in the dispute, he declared in the article, but just "limit [himself] to reading and study."

And there were confusing confessions in Roncalli's diary. During a retreat with his bishop in 1910 he had realized, "How wise, effective, and good the papal regulations are. They are intent on protecting the clergy in particular from infection by the modern (so-called modernist) erroneous teachings, which seek in a malicious and seductive manner to undermine the foundations of Catholic teaching."

Roncalli must have been terribly frightened. Was he afraid of spies rummaging through his drawers and finding his diary? The research on church history that he took refuge in during those years shows us an entirely different Roncalli, a man who has learned from history farsightedness, tolerance, and courage to engage in bold dialogue.

As far back as 1906 at the Bergamo seminary he was teaching church history, patristics (the writings of the Church Fathers), and apologetics (the scholarly defense of the Christian claim to truth). He was active in continuing education with his talks in the *Casa del Popolo* (House of the People) of Bergamo. He spoke about the relationship of the Church to modern scientific thinking, about the history of Christian pedagogy, about medieval astrology and the culture of the Renaissance. His style is said to have been graphic and marked by a cheerful composure. He often arrived late for his seminary lectures and ran panting up the stairs.

He was an enthusiastic browser in libraries and manuscript collections. In the archives of the archbishops of Milan he had discovered the reports of the visitations by St. Charles Borromeo, thirty-one thick volumes with priceless information from the counter-Reformation—and at the same time a highly concrete program for church reform based on internal renewal and intensive trust between bishop and clergy, the leadership of the Church and its spiritual personnel. Roncalli immediately decided to critically explore and then publish the documents. It became his life's work.

The last volume of the new edition, which ran to about 3,000 pages, appeared in 1958, the year he was elected pope; and at the time he quietly summed up the results. From all these large and small documents a picture emerged of a Church that shared in "poor human nature's pliability and readiness to compromise," but could still show the way to right living and acting "in a constant struggle for renewal and youth and in the holy passion for true spiritual progress."

Roncalli's thorough study of a long-dead colleague, the church historian Caesare Baronius, is also revealing. Like Borromeo, he belongs to the epoch of the counter-Reformation; his work was entirely at the service of sectarian controversy. With his *Annales Ecclesiastici* he tried to launch a pre-emptive strike on early Protestant historiography, but he avoided the usual aggressive polemics, relying exclusively on the sources and the facts.

In 1907 on the 300th anniversary of the death of Cardinal Baronius, at the seminary of Bergamo, Roncalli delivered an enigmatic festive speech. At the high water mark of the conflict over "modernism," he recalled, discreetly but unmistakably, the fundamental convictions behind scholarly work: precise investigation of the sources was necessary, "so that no one can say the Church doesn't want to hear about the light, about all the light"—and because the victory of truth, from whatever direction it comes from, will always be a victory of the Church. While Rome was taking an increasingly mistrustful view of the critical, empirical discipline of history, Roncalli joyously noted that the "astonishing advances" of this work had shed "so much new light" on the investigation of the evolution of dogma.

In the summer of 1914 the looming catastrophe seemed averted. Pius X had died at the age of seventy-nine; his successor, Benedict XV, was, as we know, a good friend of Bishop Radini-Tedeschi, and ready to support the uncomfortable activities in Bergamo. He got rid of the Roman spy-system; the Church opened up once more to the world and its unpredictable ideas.

But only a few days after Pius's death Radini-Tedeschi died too, as the mystically gifted pope had predicted. Angelo Roncalli was inconsolable; he began writing a biography of his spiritual father entitled *Il Mio Vescovo* (My Bishop) that eventually swelled to almost 500 pages. And to top it all off, he had to don his old uniform, this time in earnest. Italy had stumbled into the First World War. The troops of the sinking Austro-Hungarian monarchy inflicted frightful losses on the Italians; people began to starve. Pope Benedict's peace initiatives failed completely, because neither side was ready to give way—but in the end, in October 1918, when Italy did win a small military victory, the patriotic legends could spread their wings.

Of course, there *were* participants in the war whom the battlefields taught many lessons about politics and the interests that lay behind the general slaughter. Unless appearances are deceiving, medical corps NCO, and later Lieutenant, Roncalli was one of them. In his letters to his parents and siblings we admittedly find no political judgments, at most an occasional echo of pious fatalism: "War is war. And so, my dear Zaverio, let us always look upwards, with a generous and praying heart!" Or: "The Lord has permitted the war not to destroy us, but for our good."

But he was working out his own ideas. He asks his relatives to consider that the Germans and Austrians, who were plagued by inflation, "are suffering far more than we are." And he positively refuses to divide the world up into scapegoats and innocent victims. All sides had sinned,

and they will all, one after the other, be called to repentance. . . . But one thing is certain: the present war is a war of the rich against the poor, of the well-nourished against those who are struggling to survive, of the capitalist against the worker, and vice versa: everyone attacks and defends himself, as best he can.

In the sickbays of northern Italy where he served, keeping watch through the night, binding up torn bodies, comforting the dying, he came to know—and appreciate—the "outside" world that he had once so greatly feared. He listened to the hard men, who had previously revolted him with their brutality and smutty stories, and who now, severely wounded, had turned into desperate children. He was full of pity for their pain, and full of admiration for their spirit of self-sacrifice; because it was their homeland and their wives and children for whom they had let themselves be shot and crippled— as they had been talked into doing. "What enormous reserves of moral energy are at work in our people!" he noted, emotionally shaken. He wrote to one war widow that he bowed down before her suffering: "Ah, we are not meant for this earth!"

The battle of Caporetto alone, where Austrian and German artillery units drove Italian troops from their trenches and flung them back sixty miles behind the front, cost 45,000 dead and wounded on the Italian side; the dying lay in churches and schools, because the hospitals couldn't hold them. Medical chaplain Angelo Roncalli plunged into dark despair: "Often I could just sink to my knees and cry like a child, incapable of restraining my emotions any longer at the sight of the simple and holy dying of so many unfortunate sons of our people." In the last year of his life he still recalled: "I shall never forget the screaming of an Austrian, whose chest . . . had been torn apart by bayonet thrusts, and who was brought into the hospital at Caporetto, where I was the orderly. That picture imprinted itself still more deeply in me when I worked on my encyclical *Pacem in terris*."

The abdication of the arrogant German Kaiser Wilhelm II in November 1918 was noted by the Italian Roncalli with unconcealed satisfaction: "That's one man who liked to say *Domine, domine* (Lord, Lord!), and yet treated the Lord as an equal."

When the war was over, a new field of labor awaited him. Pope Benedict XV assigned to the forty-year-old Roncalli (who had meantime founded one of the first Italian Catholic student residences and was the spiritual advisor of the women's association of Catholic Action) the job of modernizing and internationalizing the papal missionary service, the *Propaganda Fide*. This was a responsible post that took him all across Europe.

The papal missionary service had been founded and led by the French, and hence it became isolated during the First World War. It was now to be put on a broader foundation, centralized in Rome and administered by representatives of the Church from all over the world. This plan corresponded to Pope Benedict's vision of replacing the Western-slanted hierarchy in the missionary countries with a vital native clergy. Convincing the worthy men who had been there from the start of the necessity of such a profound reorganization called for a lot of tact.

"For a hundred years we have faithfully done this work here," said one director of missions in Lyon who had grown gray in the service, "and you people in Rome want to interfere with us. Why?" Roncalli's French was not yet perfectly fluent, but he soothed the man with all the amiability of a born diplomat: "To make your good example an obligation for the other societies. To raise all the others to the level of the best!"

Now advanced to the grade of curial officer and made a monsignore, he summoned his delighted sisters Ancilla and Maria to Rome as his housekeepers. Roncalli was a thorough success in his new job. Donations to the *Propaganda Fide* doubled under his aegis. A missionary exhibit that he organized caused a sensation, not least of all because of his intensive contacts with the international press. But Roncalli the peasant's son would have been happy to remain a simple country curate or a professor of church history. Historical connections stirred his ardent interest all through his life. For just a few months he held a professorial chair at the Lateran University, an intensely traditional school, where the incautious provincial with his open-minded attitude inevitably made a striking—and unpleasant—impression.

His first semester wasn't even finished when he was recalled. In the Holy Office—the erstwhile Roman Inquisition and ancestor of the present-day Congregation for the Faith—a great deal of attention was being paid to Roncalli's sympathetic remarks about mixed marriages and his friendship with the progressive church historian Buonaiuti.

In 1958, having become pope, he was ex officio the head of the Holy Office; so as a joke he retrieved his own personal file from the archives. In it he discovered a carefully stored-away postcard sent to him decades ago by the rebel Buonaiuti, with the warning observation: "Angelo Roncalli, suspected of modernism."

Another thing that likely caused his undoing was his support for the *Partito Populare Italiano* (PPI), the party of Catholic peasants and workers founded by the Sicilian priest Luigi Sturzo. The PPI might conceivably have halted the unstoppable rise of Mussolini's Black Shirts, but the strategists in the Vatican still didn't think much of any strong political Catholicism that would have given the laity too much power. They preferred to make behind-the-scenes deals with Mussolini, who was dangling a generous compensation for the loss of the Papal States (and in the Lateran concordat of 1929 the pope actually did recover 1.75 billion lire and, along with Vatican City, his international sovereignty).

In letters to his relatives, who had long since accepted him as the intellectual head of the family, Roncalli made no attempt to hide his thoughts: at election time they should either vote for the PPI or else stay home, "and let the world go whatever way it wants. You can be sure that the welfare of Italy . . . cannot come from Mussolini, however gifted he may be. His ends may be good and right, but his means are evil, and contradict the law of the Gospel."

And in public, too, he spoke out clearly: "No, Christian Italy is not dead," he cried out in 1920 to an enthusiastic crowd at the National Eucharistic Congress in Bergamo. Catholic Action was no clerical propaganda operation, but a genuine popular cause. On the tenth anniversary of the death of Bishop Radini-Tedeschi he launched a frontal attack against the Fascists in the cathedral of Bergamo. True patriotism, he said, aims not just at military ventures and economic success, but "justice, embodied in law" and "educational freedom" (which the former grade school teacher Mussolini naturally refused to grant to Christians).

Around that time a new pope was once again installed in Rome, Pius XI. He liked the Fascists as little as he liked the Bolsheviks, yet he was opposed to clerics getting mixed up in politics and preferred the discreet paths of diplomacy to loud official protests. But now Roncalli, who knew the pope from his days in Bergamo and treasured him as "truly good and clever," began to take an increasingly skeptical view of the curia. Hence, he told a friend, "I cross its path as seldom as possible, and every time I have to go through these Vatican halls, I feel a shiver go down my back."

At around the same time, Roncalli got to know a young student chaplain, Giovanni Battista Montini, whose father—a committed journalist—had represented the PPI in parliament. Montini kept up a brave running battle with the Fascists at the University. The editorial office of the student magazine for which he wrote political articles was torched by the Black Shirts. Montini invited Roncalli to speak to his university group. Their friendship continued even when the younger man made his career in the Vatican Secretariat of State and the older man was pushed aside and landed somewhere in the Balkans. In 1963, when Montini became Roncalli's successor as pope, everybody knew he had been his heir apparent.

4

Banishment

*Wherever I go I pay more attention to what we have
in common than to what separates us.*

—Archbishop Roncalli

IT TURNED OUT TO BE A BLESSING for the Church that Professor
Roncalli came to grief in Rome and in the next few decades found
himself banished to distant diplomatic posts. It was a hard school, but
custom-made for the future pope of internal church renewal. The
drive of his charismatic personality, his clever diplomacy, and his
respect for other opinions and experiences fused ever more strongly
into the unified whole that made up his mysterious character.

When, more than three decades later, the cardinals gave him the
shoes of the fisherman, John XXIII brought the experience of a rich
life along with him. In his own assessment of this period as a Vatican
diplomat, he wrote, "Providence brought me together with people
from different religions and ideologies; it put me in touch with acute,
menacing social problems, and preserved my peace of mind and equa-
nimity for research and evaluation. While remaining unshaken in my
profession of faith and morality, I have always concerned myself more
with what unifies us than with what separates us and puts us at odds."

His first chance to do this came in Bulgaria, where he was the
first ambassador from Rome in a thousand years. He was given the
suggestive epithet "the monsignor with the motto: Let us have
understanding for one another." In February 1925, to his great surprise, he was appointed apostolic visitator in Sofia. He argued, to no

As dean of the diplomatic corps, Nuncio Roncalli gives the welcoming address at the New Year's reception for General de Gaulle in Paris, 1945. *Courtesy* Italy's News Photos, Rome

avail, that he was never trained for the diplomatic service and didn't know the least thing about Bulgaria.

But then neither did his superiors. The situation in Bulgaria, the secretary of state, Cardinal Pietro Gasparri, casually told him, was "rather confused." In 1959 Pope John was conversing with a journalist and recalled that remarkable discussion: "Everyone is apparently fighting against everyone else," Gasparri helplessly observed, "the Moslems against the Orthodox, the Greek Catholics against the Latins, and the Latins against one another. Can you go there and find out what's really going on?"

It would be only for a short time; then he'd be accepted into the official diplomatic service and sent to a quieter post. The best option would be Argentina, where there were many Italians. Roncalli accepted with a sigh, obedient as always, while his sisters Ancilla and Maria had to return in disappointment to Sotto il Monte. It was cold comfort that they could attend Roncalli's hastily arranged consecration as bishop (when he put in public appearances, he was supposed to have the same rank as the Bulgarian bishops) and be introduced to Pius XI. His parents, too, came to Rome for the event.

Roncalli told them, they shouldn't be too concerned. After all, Sofia wasn't on the other side of the world. It could be reached by direct train—the famous Orient Express—from Milan in two days. But the country that awaited him was a powder keg. Just as the titular bishop arrived in Sofia, Prime Minister General Gheorgiev was being buried after his assassination by left-wing terrorists. At the funeral service in the church of Svate Nedela another bomb exploded and killed more than a hundred people. Bulgaria hadn't won its independence until 1908, after almost five hundred years of Turkish rule. It had not only suffered heavy losses in the First World War; but it had also waged two bloody Balkan Wars against the Turks, Romanians, Serbs, and Greeks. Its economy lay in ruins; right-wing putschists and a strong Communist party boycotted the reform efforts of the middle class.

The situation of the Catholic minority was difficult too. The Orthodox established church saw the 60,000 or so Bulgarian Catholics as stateless sojourners, controlled from abroad. Their parishes formed tiny islands amid a vast Orthodox sea. The Vatican nuncio was supposed to give these herders and farmers the sense that they hadn't been forgotten by Rome, and to try to win the confidence of their skeptical leaders.

This was a delicate task, for the Catholics were also at odds with one another. The parishes that followed the Eastern rite were at least slightly integrated into society, but they were educationally and theologically primitive. In addition, they had no bishop. The "Latins" were better adapted to the cities, but the various missionary orders each had its own style, which guaranteed liturgical confusion. These were typical ghetto problems. In an old jalopy, in a shaky mule cart, or on the back of a tired nag, with a sheepskin thrown over the hard wooden saddle, the newly minted bishop traveled back and forth across the country. Worn out goat paths and dangerous mountain trails led him to the huts of his fellow Catholics, who couldn't figure out who this person visiting them was. "I tracked them down in the most distant villages," he noted, not without pride in his own toughness. "I entered their modest houses and became their neighbor." Once when he was somewhere in the middle of the mountains his driver took off, for fear of brigands. A military patrol picked up the archbishop, let him spend the night on a plank bed in a little guardhouse, and advised him to hide his pectoral cross.

Roncalli learned to appreciate the Bulgarians, their hospitality, and their music—and they began to love him. They called him *diado*, the good father. He could start building bridges between the churches—which wasn't easy, because the Bulgarian Orthodox Church behaved rather proudly and self-assuredly ever since it had broken away from the patriarchate of Constantinople. In addition it was, in a way unusual for an Eastern Church, interested in the ecumenical movement. For the Catholics of the time this was still completely unacceptable, an "invention" of the Protestants and most likely a snare of the devil, designed to undermine the true faith.

But peasants' sons from Lombardy are stubborn and patient. Besides, Roncalli considered it much more important to create a human atmosphere of open encounter—for which he had an undeniable talent—than to stage theological debates or set up negotiating committees. Peter Hebblethwaite, the ex-Jesuit from Oxford, says in his biography, *John XXIII, Pope of the Council*, a book both highly informative and full of amusing British understatement:

> Roncalli's ecumenical apprenticeship consisted in getting to know Orthodox church leaders who for the Roman curia were just a generalized abstraction—interchangeable bearded Orientals with an incomprehensible history and an unknown language.

"What a wonderful thing it is to understand and show sympathy," Roncalli wrote to his pen pal, Adelaide Coari (how he had changed!) from Sofia. On the Catholic side, one had so much to learn about the Orthodox—and you had to let yourself be driven by love of neighbor, "so as to hasten the day when the brothers would return to the unity of the Church. Do you follow me? Through charity—rather than through theological discussions."

His vision of church unity still sounds a bit like the repentant return of sons gone astray; but perhaps he didn't mean it that way. To another conversation partner he explained that one had to promote every single path to fraternization between Catholics and Orthodox "that can lead all of us more profoundly to the pure sources of Christian religious life." All of us.

A young Orthodox Bulgarian man wanted to join the Catholic Church and become a priest. He may have displayed a somewhat aggressive religious fervor, as converts will do. In any case Archbishop Roncalli wrote him a letter bidding him stay calm:

> The Catholics and the Orthodox are not enemies, but brothers. We have the same faith, we share the same sacraments and, in particular, the same Eucharist. We are divided by several misunderstandings about the divine institution of the Church of Jesus Christ. Those who caused these misunderstandings have been dead for centuries. Let's drop the old disputes and work, each one of us in his own field, to make our brothers good by showing them a good example. You will learn a great deal in the sem-

inary, above all, love for Jesus, the spirit of the apostolate and of sacrifice. Later we shall meet, even though we have taken different paths, in a union of the churches, in order to form together the one true Church of our Lord Jesus Christ.

In Bulgaria Angelo Roncalli undoubtedly went through the most important learning experience of his life till then. He met countless worthy men and women who belonged to another denomination. He had to admit that strange rites and religious practices not accepted by Rome could be a sure way to God. He suffered because he couldn't stand together at the altar with clerics and bishops whom he liked and respected. But he also saw that the classic method of "union" with Rome had often only led to new divisions.

Roncalli observed, learned—and felt utterly miserable. He would have so much liked to be a pastor in Bergamo, he wrote his friend Don Clienze; he would have happily taught religion classes, heard confessions, helped young clerics in the seminary. Instead, he was

> all day long . . . busy with the typewriter or with burdensome affairs, between many difficulties and nasty digs. Among people who also belong to Jesus Christ and, rightly speaking, to the Catholic Church, but who in no way have the 'sensus Christi' [the sense of Christ]. . . . Always in contact with the so-called great ones of the world, but troubled by the pettiness of their minds with regard to the supernatural. Carefully preparing things from which so much good is to come forth, and then witnessing the fragility of human hopes.

Roncalli does go on to say: "In spite of all that, dear Don Clienze, one lives in peace; because in the end success goes to those who do the will of the Lord with real magnanimity [*magno corde*], who take everything well and obey lovingly." But that was by no means always enough to comfort him. He had been told that Bulgaria would only be an intermediate stop. But the interim dragged on for years without Rome's giving the slightest hint of intending to put him to any new use.

The home office on the Tiber paid scarcely any attention to his ideas and well-informed suggestions—which came down to having the Catholic Church in the Balkans stand a bit more on its own two feet, and to slackening Rome's short leash, for instance by naming a native-born bishop for the parishes of the Slavic rite. Roncalli found it extremely upsetting that these communities were "administered" by apostolic visitors located in Macedonia and Thrace, in other words abroad. His candidate was a thirty-four-year-old religious priest named Stefan Kurtev, whom he actually managed to get approved in Rome—although only after higher-ups took a year to think it over.

On the other hand, the seminary for the future generation of Bulgarian priests that Roncalli urgently recommended, so that the Catholic Church could set down stronger roots in the country, never became a reality, even though he had already bought an appropriate site for it. He advised giving more freedom to the Uniate Catholics of the Eastern rite, who were bound to Rome; but that, too, fell on deaf ears. Once more the missionaries of the Latin rite were up in arms against the idea, and naturally they had powerful spokesmen in the Vatican.

This priest, who was otherwise so modest, obedient, and self-critical, now expressed his bitter disappointment over his experiences with Roman centralism. "It's a form of insult and humiliation that I never expected and that hurts me a great deal," he confided to his diary in 1926, while making his annual retreat in the monastery of St. Paul. The frustration in his new post had come not from the Bulgarians, "but from the central organs of the Church's administration." To his sisters Ancilla and Maria he wrote—perhaps to comfort them, because they were no doubt still hankering for their splendid old housekeeping job—that he was glad to leave Rome again.

It frustrated me to have to join in witnessing all those wretched little human ploys. Everyone is trying to get a position and make a career, and they're busy chattering about it. What a degradation of priestly life . . .

Once he is said to have complained or justified himself in a twenty-page letter (unfortunately lost) to some curial body. Pope Pius XI was shown the letter and dryly noted, "Look, the lamb [meaning Roncalli] can get angry too." They were just completely different natures, the pope and his nuncio. In October 1930 Catholic Italy rejoiced when Bulgaria's King Boris III married Princess Giovanna, the daughter of King Victor Emmanuel, in Assisi. With a papal dispensation, to be sure, because Boris was Orthodox, the couple had been obliged to sign a promise to bring up their children as Catholics. It was a fairytale wedding and had great political importance for both countries.

But the pope soon had reason to be enraged: a week after the marriage the royal pair married for the second time—this time in the Orthodox rite, at the Alexander Nevsky Cathedral back home in Sofia. Pius delivered a furious speech before the assembled College of Cardinals, accused the king of breaking his word, and the Romans soon found a scapegoat: Apostolic Visitator Roncalli who hadn't kept his eyes open.

In the first place, Roncalli was completely innocent of the charge, and secondly he behaved much more calmly than the pope. Everything depended on how one interpreted the ceremony in the Orthodox cathedral: as an affront to Rome or as an attempt by the monarch to pacify his divided country. King Boris had himself been baptized a Catholic and had gone over to Orthodoxy. He had to avoid anything that might cause the leadership of the Orthodox Church to doubt his loyalty. And then too, weren't the Orthodox sacraments fully valid from the Catholic standpoint?

Three years later, when the royal couple had their first child baptized—contrary to the agreement—according to the Orthodox rite, another storm broke out in Rome. Roncalli had to hand the monarch a sharp note of protest that spoke of the "pain of the Holy Father and of all good Catholics"; and for a year afterwards he was no longer received in the royal court. But he knew how to pour oil on troubled waters. He invited the unhappy queen to attend his mass instead of in the Catholic parish church, to avoid any fuss. He also gave her a marvelously beautiful missal. Behind closed doors, he chided the Vatican Secretariat of State for agreeing to any unrealistic promises made by

King Boris, because the Bulgarian Orthodox would never have gone along with the heir to the throne being baptized as a Catholic.

Is it true, as rumor has it, that Pius XI punished Archbishop Roncalli, now fallen into disfavor, by making him kneel down before him for three-quarters of an hour? Or did the pope, as others claim, "privately" forgive him? One thing is certain: from now on, Roncalli was taken seriously even less than before. Evidently he was too naïve for the diplomatic business and much too softhearted to withstand harsh ecclesiastical-political conflicts. Granted, he was given a fine new title, apostolic delegate, instead of visitator; but he didn't get the archbishopric of Milan, as people had been whispering he would.

French President Vincent Auriol places the cardinal's biretta on the newly appointed Cardinal Roncalli on January 15, 1953. *Courtesy* Giovanni XXIII

5

The Balkan Years

Whoever forsakes the old way for the new knows
what he is losing, but not what he will find.
—Italian Proverb

IT'S NOT QUITE CLEAR why Pius XI transferred Roncalli, who had-
n't exactly covered himself with glory, to Istanbul in 1935, as apostolic delegate for Greece and Turkey. This was a far more complicated field of operations than Bulgaria. Perhaps people in the
Vatican had, after all, recognized how valuable the good feelings
were that the presumably naive but charismatic Roncalli managed
to evoke. When he had arrived in Sofia ten years before, scarcely
anyone had taken notice of him. And now they were giving him a
moving send-off, in which even representatives from the royal
house and the Orthodox Church took part.

They were all enthusiastic when Roncalli announced that he
had given back "his" diocese of Areopolis and would now be
allowed, with Rome's permission, to call himself the archbishop of
Mesembria. That title came from an ancient harbor town on the
Bulgarian Black Sea coast, whose precious churches combine
Bulgarian and Byzantine stylistic traits. Titular bishops, who are in
charge of no existing diocese, are assigned some ruined city from
Christian antiquity. In Roncalli's case that was Areopolis, in the
then-British protectorate of Palestine, somewhere between the
Dead Sea and Red Sea. But he preferred to take with him a souvenir
of Bulgaria in his title when he left the country he had come to love.

In his departure sermon he told, as he was wont, about the Irish custom of putting a lit candle in the window at Christmastime—as a signal to the wandering Holy Family that they could find shelter there. "Wherever I may go," Roncalli promised,

> When a Bulgarian goes by my door, even by night and even if he be a poor beggar, he will see that sort of candle burning in my window. Knock! Knock! You won't be asked whether or not you are Catholic. It's enough that you are a brother from Bulgaria. Come on in! The arms of a brother will receive you, and the warm heart of a friend will make the day a feast day.

Being a papal nuncio in Turkey or in Greece, soberly considered, was just another diplomatic dead-end, far from the centers of world politics and Catholic intellectual life. But it was also a task for Hercules. In a traditionally dyed-in-the-wool Islamic country like Turkey, a Vatican observer must in any case have felt like an uninvited guest. But, beyond that, ever since Kemal Atatürk's coming to power in 1923, religion was being driven from public life. And if the mullahs had nothing more to say, then Christian clergymen, who were considered foreign agents, positively had to sink into oblivion.

The new Turkey was experimenting with all sorts of Western achievements that might win the approval of a Vatican envoy: introducing the Gregorian calendar, abolishing polygamy, granting equal rights to women, adopting the Swiss civil code and the Italian penal code. But Atatürk's government also established strict separation of church and state, and denied all religious communities any influence on schools and the education of children. Hardly had the Vatican delegate arrived in Istanbul—where he forfeited his diplomatic status because Turkey had no ties to the Vatican—when the Catholic church newspaper was banned, and a short time later a law forbade the wearing of religious dress in public. The Muslims had to give up their fezzes, the Catholic priests their soutanes. Roncalli didn't take such harassment too tragically; the word of God could be preached in trousers as well as in a cassock. Unfortunately, in his unfamiliar civilian outfit he also lost some of his dignity. The malicious Peter

Hebblethwaite says that in photos that have been preserved the arch-bishop with his derby and dark suit looks "just like a businessman from Lombardy who has had a hard time resisting the pasta."

But Turkey's official atheism wasn't the only problem. Relations between the 35,00 Catholics and the 100,000 Orthodox in Istanbul were plagued by jealousy and power plays; and once again the various Catholic rites were at odds with one another: Latins (with a French accent), Syrians, Chaldeans, Armenians, and Jacobites all protected their own rites and traditions.

The situation in Greece seemed no less complicated, and the new nuncio residing in Istanbul was also responsible for Greece— as a sort of traveling representative. Like Turkey, Greece was caught in a crisis-ridden transformation, in this case from a short-lived republic to an authoritarian monarchy. In 1936 General Metaxas sent the Parliament home and ruled by emergency decree with the help of the army. The Catholic communities were very strictly controlled and oppressed. In particular the Greek Orthodox established church viewed the Byzantine-rite Catholics, who were scarcely distinguishable from them in externals, as a dangerous foreign body. A law was being prepared to withdraw the state's recognition of all marriages not solemnized according to the Orthodox rite.

In addition, when they dispatched Roncalli, the strategists in Rome had apparently ignored the fact that the Greeks viewed the Bulgarians as their enemies, and that a Vatican representative coming directly from Sofia would be bound to be met with distrust. Sending an Italian was also clumsy because people still had unpleasant memories of the Italian bombardment of Corfu in 1923; and Mussolini was just then preparing to occupy Albania—and thus threaten Greece.

Given this inextricable tangle of problems, another man might have crawled into a monastery, occasionally celebrated a nice mass with a small group of associates, and regularly but not too often sent elegiac reports to Rome about how things were going. But the chronically underestimated Roncalli used even the icy winds blowing through Istanbul to learn something. Admittedly, here he was at what looked like the end of the Catholic world; but with his broad experience, he was way ahead of his superiors ensconced in their Vatican palaces.

When he compared Turkey under Atatürk and the Orthodox "theocracy of Greece" with its manifold hindrances to Catholic communities, Angelo Roncalli had to admit that the Church could remain alive even in an officially atheistic state. Indeed, he thought the loss of privileges and protective measures from the government could even be liberating. In Istanbul, where all Christian churches saw themselves exposed to the same government attacks, free and impartial ecumenical contacts necessarily sprang up. Roncalli learned that the answer to an anti-religious environment had to come not from building a ghetto, but could also be based on dialogue between churches facing a common challenge.

With strenuous efforts the Italian tried to break down the barriers of mistrust in both countries and to get some air for the Catholics to breathe. Fortunately, Roncalli discovered that his banishment to Istanbul—before Atatürk it had been called Constantinople—made it possible to take a step back into the world of pastoral care. That was because in the event of conflict between churches the pope's vicar is allowed to dispense justice like a bishop, and with Roncalli's temperament this sort of arbitration inevitably took on a rather therapeutic form. His manner was more reminiscent of a brother and friend rather than of an envoy from military headquarters.

In the retreat he made in 1940 on the Bosporus "composure" was the quality he swore to seek, "a greater readiness for understanding and forbearance" and striving to make calm judgments:

I want to alertly pay heed to remaining simple in word and demeanor and to avoid posing. But at the same time something of the dignity and lovable refinement of an old bishop should shine forth to everyone, from a man who spreads about him an air of venerability, wisdom, and friendliness.

At the time Roncalli was fifty-nine and he already loved the solemn language of aging clerics. Among his duties was the attentive visitation of parishes and monasteries, but he admonished all his coworkers in the Church's hierarchy to attend to such inspections respectfully and delicately, "on tiptoe," as he put it. On the centenary of the founding of the Little Sisters of the Poor he turned the occasion—despite the nuns' objections—into a grand festival that caught even the public's eye. And whenever an old religious was lay to rest, he himself delivered the eulogy. He did the same when the sacristan of the Catholic cathedral, a man who had served long and honorably, died in the Jeremiah Hospital of Istanbul.

Another reason why the Catholic enclaves in Turkey seemed like settlements of a foreign power was that scarcely any priests could speak really fluent Turkish—something that the watchful Vatican had long been critical of. But Roncalli introduced concrete steps to change this. He sent out official documents exclusively in Turkish; now and then he had the Gospel read at mass in the national language, and recommended using Turkish at eucharistic devotions, where the prayers were usually held in Latin, Italian, or French. The people who listened to his sermons noticed that, in keeping with the Creed, he spoke of the "one holy, Catholic and apostolic Church," but dropped the "Roman" that his confreres liked to put in. These small signals often had a stunning effect; more than once hard-line Catholics marched out of church, insulted when Roncalli used the seldom-heard vernacular in the liturgy. But in the Foreign Ministry in Ankara people began to feel respect for "the Italian."

He showed unusual tact. In a brief *mandement* during Lent (a "pastoral letter" would have struck him as too provocative) Roncalli called for prayers for this "strong and powerful nation that is seeking paths to higher development." In 1937, when he finally dared to call on Undersecretary Numan Rifat Menemencoglu in the Foreign Ministry, the latter amiably but firmly pointed out to him that distance from every kind of religion was a fundamental principle of the Turkish state and represented "the guarantee of our freedom"; and so a spiritual power like the Vatican was for Ankara "certainly respectable, but alien to us." To which Roncalli replied,

> I understand. That does not prevent the spiritual power from rejoicing over the rise of Turkey and from discovering in its new constitution some basic principles of Christianity . . . I am an

optimist. Everywhere I go I pay more attention to what we have in common than to what separates us. Since we agree about the principles of natural law, we could also travel together for a good stretch of the way.

He showed the same tact when he met with the other Christian confessions. The mere fact that such meetings took place at all was a novelty. He was the first Catholic in ages to enter the Phanar, the official residence of the Greek Orthodox patriarch of Constantinople. With the humility of a pilgrim and the hungry interest of a church historian, he visited spiritual centers of Orthodoxy such as Mount Athos. In his sermons he liked to go back to the fathers of the Eastern Church, with whom he had a remarkable familiarity ever since his brief period as a Roman professor. In Istanbul he amazed foreign scholars with the hitherto unknown Byzantine inscriptions he had discovered and deciphered in the course of his walks through the Old City.

In 1939 there was another change at the helm of the Church; Eugenio Pacelli, who took the name of Pius XII, had been cardinal secretary of state and Roncalli's immediate boss; and so his representative in Istanbul declared himself very satisfied. At the *Te Deum* sung for the happily concluded papal election an envoy from the ecumenical patriarch was present—a gesture that turned heads. There was even more astonishment when Roncalli expressed his thanks in the Phanar and was warmly embraced by the Greek Orthodox patriarch.

On Pentecost, 1942 the Catholic world celebrated the 25th anniversary of Pope Pius' consecration as a bishop. In Istanbul Roncalli preached enigmatically about the "equal commission" that all the apostles had received from Jesus. Naturally, he didn't forget to mention the "outstanding place" that Peter occupied, but he deliberately did not call the pope "the vicar of Christ," simply "the bishop of Rome"—the term used before the Great Schism.

These were small steps, discreet but clear gestures: naturally, the walls that had been built up between the Christian churches over the centuries couldn't be torn down with a single thrust; and the

Angelo Roncalli enters Venice on the Grand Canal as
patriarch on March 15, 1953. *Courtesy* Loris Capovilla,
"L'ite missa est di papa Giovanni"

archbishop realistically conceded that. But, he said, "I'm trying to pull out a brick here and there." His image of the Church was coming closer and closer to the vision with which he would later, as pope sweep away Christians of all confessions. In 1940 he again made his retreat, among the Sisters of Our Lady of Mount Sion in Terapia on the Bosporus; and he noted that for him the Church was no "historical monument from the past," but a "living institution." Its founding had been steadily progressing for two thousand years, and everyone had to lend a hand.

In October 1940 Italian and later German troops invaded Greece. Sixty thousand people were executed; millions were driven out of their homes. Famine soon raged throughout the country. Once again it's not easy to determine what Roncalli felt and thought at the time. As a diplomat he maintained an iron silence—and helped with a great deal of energy and imagination wherever he could. As an Italian Catholic he also strove to keep silent—but he felt inwardly torn: "Nature makes me hope for the success of my dear country," he confided to a Monsignore Guillois in Istanbul, "but grace fills me more than ever with the desire to seek peace and to fight for it." Guillois was French; and the Italians had just then declared war on France. Both men were close to tears as they gave one another the kiss of peace.

When Mussolini attacked Abyssinia—a people with a high Christian culture—the Vatican had received the news in silence; and some bishops had greeted it with patriotic joy: along with bombs and poison gas, their commentary ran, the African savages were, after all, getting a dose of Western civilization; and the penniless southern Italians who wanted to emigrate now finally knew where they could build a better future.

In his letters to Sotto il Monte Roncalli twisted and turned looking for a clear position. The whole world, he wrote, was "topsy-turvy," and when one tried to judge such complicated questions, one could easily miscalculate. In any case it wasn't the soldiers' fault. "The ones responsible are the leaders. They are the ones with the thick skulls, and they're all alike. But then he unexpectedly quoted an old fable: "The big fish would like to gobble up the smaller fish,

while the smaller one says the ocean is big and belongs to everyone."
His sympathies were obviously not with Italy the predator. And during the above-mentioned retreat he clearly realized that, "The world is poisoned by an unhealthy nationalism based on blood and race, which flatly contradicts the Gospel." Another time he called the war "a slaughterhouse": all sides would have to make immense sacrifices. "But what pain for so many mothers, brides and innocent children!"

Around this time a remarkable friendship developed between the archbishop and Franz von Papen, who in 1939 had been sent as Germany's ambassador to Turkey. Turkey was important for keeping the Axis's right flank clear in a war with Russia. Roncalli probably preferred to see in Papen a good bourgeois Catholic who had tried, first as chancellor of the Reich and then as Hitler's colleague in the cabinet, to civilize the Führer and his bloodthirsty gang. Hadn't he resigned from the government after the Röhm putsch, the "Night of the Long Knives"? To be sure, the Vatican resented Papen's contacts with the paramilitary "Stahlhelm" (steel helmet) units and his activities in Vienna, where he had been busily involved with preparations for the Anschluß of Austria to Hitler's Germany.

Papen seems to have used Roncalli to keep the skeptical Vatican favorably disposed to his side. After a long conversation with the ambassador, Roncalli reported eagerly to Rome that if the "robust and enthusiastic forces" of the Catholic Church would participate in the task of national construction, it might well be "that after the war Catholicism could become the 'formative principle' of the new German social order." Of course, the archbishop also mentioned that he had asked Papen about the pagan foundations of Nazi ideology and had alluded to Hitler's notorious tendency to violate treaties.

Even here the goodhearted Roncalli doesn't seem to have been too naïve, though he never doubted the value of the German nonaggression pact with the Soviet Union. Perhaps too it was premature to provide Papen's cultural attaché, Kurt von Lersner, with a letter of recommendation to Roncalli's old friend Montini in the Secretariat of State. Lersner had hinted that powerful forces, above all in the German army, were interested in ending the war; so perhaps the pope could play a mediating role here. It later turned out that the austere Protestant Lersner actually *was* an opponent of Hitler and did want a different kind of Germany. Roncalli kept up his friendship with Papen, and in 1946 he helped save him from the gallows in Nuremberg. He wrote to the judges that he didn't want to get involved in a political judgment of the man, but they might want to consider the fact that Papen had given him a good deal of money from his espionage fund to save the lives of persecuted individuals.

Archbishop Roncalli was referring to the highly effective relief services that he had founded in Istanbul—without managing to quiet his continual bad conscience over having to keep silent. Back in the very first days of the war when the Germans occupied Warsaw, Roncalli took steps to support Polish refugees. Later, along with the Red Cross, he organized a clearing-house for information about POWs—which took a bit of artistry since a faction in the Roman curia viewed the Red Cross as a hated rival. He visited wounded German and English soldiers in the hospitals. Ever since a severe earthquake had devastated Bulgaria in 1928 he had learned how to organize relief measures quickly and non-bureaucratically. In those days Apostolic Visitator Roncalli had gone immediately to the scene of the disaster, and within three days he had gotten food and woolen blankets from Rome for the homeless.

In the fall of 1941 the misery in Greece reached its zenith; every day something like a thousand people were dying of hunger. The civilian population was waiting in desperation for 360,000 tons of wheat—aid shipments from abroad—that had already been loaded in the harbor of Haifa. But the English had blocked the Greek harbors, to cut off supplies to the German and Italian troops. Roncalli made skillful attempts to free up the vitally needed deliveries by bringing in the Orthodox Metropolitan of Athens and his contacts with the Greek government in exile in London. He failed (although some of his biographers deny that), but the Vatican, warned by Roncalli, sent food, condensed milk, and medicine that the archbishop distributed through sixteen relief centers. When an Athenian businessman, who had hoarded foodstuffs and in the face of the dreadful famine had been demanding astronomical prices for flour and dried vegetables, the normally gentle Monsignore is said to have threatened him personally with a beating if he didn't at once start doing business honestly. The story was attested to by Roncalli's secretary, who was on hand when the enraged archbishop burst into the store.

Because he resided in neutral Turkey, Roncalli could also do more than others for the Jews who were being hounded from country to country. In September 1940 one group of refugees from the Warsaw ghetto had brought him the first reports about the concentration camps and the massacres carried out by the *Einsatzgruppen*. More and more persecuted men and women wanted to travel through the Balkans to Palestine, where the British mandatory forces often blocked their entry.

Roncalli worked with Jewish refugee organizations, with Chaim Barlas from the Jewish Agency for Palestine, and later with Chief Rabbi Israel Herzog of Jerusalem. He passed on their requests to the Vatican—including the wish to declare loudly and clearly that the Church's help for threatened Jews should be viewed as a godly work of mercy. The Vatican reacted coolly to this, as we know. Roncalli was shocked: "Poor children of Israel," he wrote to a correspondent, "every day I hear their groans around me. They are Jesus' relatives and countrymen." He scraped the bottom of his own resources and found a way to save from the death camps thousands of Slovakian Jews who were detained in Hungary or Bulgaria by signing their transit visas to Palestine. And then there was Papen's pot of gold, which paid for food and clothing.

In the fall of 1943 when the Vatican began to play a more active role and helped many Italian Jews to flee by ship to Palestine from the German occupying forces, Roncalli voiced some odd criticism to the secretary of state, Cardinal Maglione: By engaging in such "simple and noble compassion" the Holy See was exposing itself to the suspicion of "making an indirect contribution to the realization of the messianic dream" and to the restoration of the kingdoms of Israel and Juda. But when it came to lending a hand and saving lives, Roncalli had no such theological scruples: in 1944 he managed to get Rumanian Jews, who were candidates for Auschwitz, on board Turkish ships to Palestine. Through Vatican representatives in Hungary and Romania he provided countless persecuted persons with the often ineffective but sometimes useful immigration certificates issued by the Jewish Agency for Palestine. This gave rise to the legend that Roncalli handed out false baptismal certificates to save the lives of Jews.

In July, 1943 when the Allies landed in Sicily, and Italy signed a truce in September, when German troops occupied Rome and the partisan campaign against the Nazis began, Roncalli, for all his concerns, was relieved. He wrote to his brother Giovanni back home that the new political phase, which had been launched without great upheavals, showed "that in Italy there is still such a rich supply of healthy common sense and human dignity, which counts for more than any victory won with brutal weapons."

In Rome, as usual, people didn't think much of him. His old friends had long since moved up to better posts on the clerical ladder and wondered why the sympathetic Lombard was still stuck in the Balkans. Roncalli's reports and suggestions had little resonance. Back in Sofia he had advised a friend not to mention his name if he wanted to be successful in Rome. The issue being discussed was settling an order of nuns in Bulgaria, and Roncalli had observed: "It would be best not to let word get around that the idea comes from me . . ."

Now, ten years later, he once again noted sadly in his diary:

It's as if I were removed from everything, even from any thought of getting ahead. I have nothing to my credit, nor do I feel any impatience. But it hurts me that there could be so great a gap between my judgment of the situation here and the way the same things are viewed in Rome. This is my only real cross. I want to bear it in humility, ready to satisfy my highest superiors, because this—and nothing else—is dear to my heart. I will always tell the truth, but gently, and keep silent about everything that I feel I have suffered by way of injustice or insults. . . . The Lord sees everything and will do me justice.

This is one of the very few complaints in his diary amid all the resolutions to stay serene. And even in his correspondence disappointment flares up very seldom, for example when he says he envies an old schoolmate for being able to engage in pastoral work full-time: "How poor the life of a bishop or priest is who's forced to be merely a diplomat or bureaucrat!"

"*Questo a capito niente*" (he just doesn't get it) gruffly commented Monsignore Domenico Tardini in the Vatican, when yet another letter arrived from Istanbul with detailed news reports that Hitler's henchman Papen had passed on to Archbishop Roncalli. As director of the foreign department of the Secretariat of State, Tardini was Roncalli's immediate contact. He was considered unconditionally loyal to the pope, politically experienced, but socially unpleasant: curt, arrogant, sometimes rather callous.

But it really wasn't so easy to decide whether Angelo Roncalli, who was always ready to talk to all sides, who gave his heartfelt kindness without distinction, was dangerously naïve or exceedingly wise. "I am," he wrote his family, "more for the iron that bends than for the iron that breaks." Later in Paris his nephew Battista, whom he had guided to the priesthood, asked him admiringly—and perhaps a bit mistrustfully too—how he was able to keep his footing on the slippery dance floor of diplomacy while remaining true to himself. Roncalli's answer: "By always telling the truth, although the others suspect the opposite."

Angelo the sly peasant was never as obedient and predictable as many people thought. He smiled and chatted—and still managed to keep his secret. He seemed gentle and lovable, he valued discussion, he took weird arguments seriously—and at the crucial moment he knew exactly what he wanted. He made a game of disappointing the case-hardened expectations of the world around him. One day he sat with the critical Jesuit and newspaper editor Robert Rouquette and read to him, with relish, a whole chapter from Giovanni Papini's *Letters to People Who Call Themselves Christian*—a series of malicious remarks about Catholics who thought of themselves as modern. Then again he immediately ordered Rouquette to correct the caricatures of contemporary French theology being spread by conservatives in Rome.

Roncalli's frank correspondence with the ecumenically minded and socially committed Adelaida Coari speaks volumes. He had become acquainted with this Catholic woman, who was just his age, when he was secretary to the bishop of Bergamo. She fought to get women a voice in politics and the Church as well as for a strong Christian labor movement. Cardinal Merry del Val, Pius X's secretary of state, had written a circular letter decreeing that women, "even respected and pious women," were never to be allowed to speak at Catholic congresses and in Catholic associations. Undaunted, Adelaida founded a Christian Democratic Women's League in Milan and an independent newspaper. Crushed by resistance from archconservative circles, she began to work in teacher training and as an inspector of public schools.

When Roncalli was shunted off to Sofia, he begged his correspondent not to give up and to work for the Catholic cause "outside the usual framework." Because, he said, whatever was going on outside the officially recognized possibilities was still part of the Church. Roncalli called the attention of the important Jesuit paper *Civiltá Cattolica* to this interesting woman. Adelaida—who outlived Roncalli by three years and who corresponded with him until his death—left behind some informative notes about the relationship of Pope John to his Vatican milieu. It deeply wounded him, she says, how little the eighth commandment, "Thou shalt not bear false witness against thy neighbor," counted there.

The letters that Roncalli wrote to his relatives back in Sotto il Monte naturally deal with different subjects and cares. As the acknowledged head of the family, he sends advice, serves up praise and blame, and hints that things aren't exactly rosy in his little episcopal palace: "I'm sending you a 100 lire note so that you'll think of me today. It is, so to speak, the last bullet in my belt. . . . This year I've fired off a few too many."

Back when Angelo still lived at home, the family had left the narrow house he was born in and moved to the Colombera, a former custodian's estate nearby. Forty years later, with help from Angelo and a bank loan, his father was able to buy the estate and ten adjoining acres of land. It took him forty years to pay off the mortgage; it would take another twenty years to cancel the last vestige of debt.

"Have you bought the heater? Does it work?" Angelo inquired in January 1926. He knew how cheerless the "winter of the poor" was, and he still bore the scars of chilblains on his hands from the frosts of his childhood. He asked about the state of repairs on the Columbera, recommended painting the staircase "a nice pearl-color" and providing its door with frosted glass, "expanding the inside of the toilet so that it gets light from one half of the window, while the other half gives light to the entryway staircase." He busied himself with the slightest details, advising his family to set up two separate kitchens and promising to help out financially: "With so many daughters-in-law in the house, and with all those children, there are bound to be continuous disagreements." After a devastating storm he comforted his parents with the words: "We are always in good hands," but he also sent them 1,000 lire, which he had to borrow. "Let's not complain! It's meant to be. I bless you all from the heart, great and small." He is warmly interested in their raising silkworms (income from this enabled father Giovanni to get the mortgage on the Colombera). And he wants to know what his faithful sisters Ancilla and Maria have to say about his plans to build a chicken coop in the garden of his official residence in Istanbul.

He reports unhappily about the modest success of his attempt to stay on a diet: mornings he has a caffe latte with a little bread and fruit, at noon a solid meal, "but with not much bread or wine." In the evenings he has soup, vegetables, some bread and fruit. "I've got to cut down somewhat, to build up my resistance, now that my age is going downhill." But his efforts had few results, and his sisters in the kitchen wondered: "For a man who's as fat as a parish priest, he eats like a sparrow. It must be all those books and newspapers he swallows!" Angelo's simple words hit the right note when he congratulates his sister Assunta on her grandchild and asks her not to let herself be eaten up by care:

Just think how much trouble your children cost you, and now they all have jobs. Isn't that a great grace! And I have already been gone from Bergamo and home for thirty years. Do you think my life was and is a pleasure? This may be enough to tell you, dear Assunta, that when all is said and done we don't live free from cares here, and that if we take them upon ourselves, they redound to our advantage for the better life that awaits us all. Your Giovanni is already there and rejoices now over the suffering he went through. How beautiful the feast of St. John must be for him in paradise, along with Angelino and all our beloved dead!

Roncalli wrote this letter on the eve of the name day of Assunta's deceased husband Giovanni (John). Angelino had been his nephew, the son of his eldest brother; he too had wanted to be a priest, but at the age of twelve he had died after catching a bad cold. Another nephew had been fatally wounded on the Greek-Italian front. Meanwhile Roncalli's parents were dead as well—his father died in 1935 at the age of eighty-one, his mother in 1939 at eighty-five. Their son hadn't been able to come to either funeral. Around the time of his father's death the church crisis in Turkey had reached its climax; and when his mother died, Pius XI had just died in Rome, and Roncalli couldn't get out of all the official condolence visits and ceremonies.

She would have so much liked to have her Angelo by her side one more time; when he wrote to her about the death of the pope explaining there was no way he could leave Istanbul just then, she murmured resignedly, "I understand, he really can't come. Now let's hope the Lord will let me stay here a little longer; and if not, I'll obey his will, and we'll see one another again in heaven."

6

Proving Himself

My windows are wide open, and my ears are ready
to listen. But on many topics my lips are sealed.

—*Angelo Giuseppe Roncalli*

BACK IN THE VATICAN, over the course of twenty long years, the one-time bishop's secretary from the working class diocese of Bergamo had apparently been forgotten. But in December, 1944, as World War II was drawing to a close, Pius XII suddenly transferred the sixty-three-year-old Roncalli overnight to the most important coordinating position of papal diplomacy: as nuncio to Paris. Not that the curia's appreciation for Roncalli was any greater than before. When he remarked that he was surprised by the promotion, a high-ranking prelate brusquely told him, "We're all surprised by it. That one did it all by himself!" The dismissive wave of the hand was aimed at the study of Pius XII.

Roncalli himself knew that he was only the second choice: the candidate favored by Vatican bureaucrats, the Argentinian nuncio Fietta, had turned down the move to Paris for reasons of health. With a bitter smile he quoted a line from a Renaissance poet, "*Ubi deficiunt equi, trottant aselli*" (where horses are lacking, the asses get to trot). Apart from the fact that he could hardly be enthusiastic about a promotion that involved even less pastoral work than previous jobs, he was catapulted into the hotbed of political intrigue and diplomatic gambits that he so much hated.

Coming when it did, the promotion was like being sent on a sui-

Pope Pius XII and Cardinal Roncalli in Rome: predecessor
and successor, type and conter-type, majestic figure of light
and earthbound conversationalist. *Courtesy* Felici

cide mission. Thanks to its splendid religious history, France was still known in Catholic circles by the honorific title, "Eldest Daughter of the Church," but relations between the government and the Church hierarchy had reached rock bottom. While many nameless Christians had fought in the Resistance against the German army of occupation, the majority of their bishops had been faithful supporters of Marshall Pétain, who administered Vichy France in close collaboration with Nazi Germany. In Pétain's authoritarian regime classic pre-conciliar Catholicism saw its dream come true. "France," the otherwise extremely sensitive poet Paul Claudel exulted, "has been set free from the yoke of the anti-Catholic party—professors, lawyers, Jews and Freemasons."

To be sure, closeness to the Vichy regime didn't necessarily mean approval of Nazism. Pétain had been legally appointed head of state; and when in 1942 the Germans began to deport French Jews to the death camps, some hitherto very pliant bishops turned into real lions. Cardinal Gerlier, for example, who back in 1940 had proclaimed, *"Pétain, c'est la France!"* ran ingenious rescue operations for the Jews of Lyon.

General Charles de Gaulle, who in 1940 had set up a French government-in-exile in London and later had agitated against the German occupying forces from his base in North Africa, marched into Paris as a liberator in August of 1944. At an audience in the Vatican he demanded that Pius XII dismiss Nuncio Valerio Valeri, who was seriously handicapped by his close contacts with the Vichy government, as well as thirty bishops likewise accused of collaboration. With his keen sense of power, Pius XII naturally made trouble at first: What would happen if any political faction that happened to be at the helm could decide who was to fill spiritual posts?

But with time the curia realized that if Valeri were kept on, the entire French Church would be subjected to a brutal and life-threatening test. Meanwhile it was already December, and time was pressing: If the position of nuncio remained vacant, then at the New Year's day reception the oldest member of the *Corps diplomatique* would convey the members' greetings. At the moment this would be Soviet ambassador Bogomolov, and not its traditional dean, the papal nuncio. That sort of disgrace had to be prevented.

And so on December 2 a telegram was sent to Joseph Fietta in Buenos Aires; and after he vehemently refused, another wire was sent on December 5 to Angelo Roncalli in Istanbul. On December 27 Roncalli left Turkey. He arrived in Rome the next day—after half a dozen intermediate stops, and on December 29 he was received by the pope. At 10 a.m. on December 30 he left Rome on a French government aircraft; he landed at two in the afternoon at a military airport near Paris, presented himself that evening to Foreign Minister Bidault, and on January 1, 1945 managed to deliver the New Year's address that had caused all the commotion. An amusing legend claims that he simply read the text prepared by the ambassador from Moscow, to the great delight of the Soviets; but in fact the speech had been written by experienced Vatican officials.

Nuncio Roncalli, the second choice: Most insiders supposed that Pius XII had been so vexed by the demands from Paris and the forced recall of Monsignor Valeri that out of pure revenge he sent the most incompetent follow-up candidate, " 'the peasant' among his diplomats, a man he could hardly have liked." The pope's anger, people speculated, was directed at the intellectual upheaval that was rumbling through French Catholicism at the time, a movement that the authoritarian Pius XII inevitably viewed as schismatic: guidelines for theology and pastoral care were to be laid down in Rome and nowhere else. Period.

One of the thousand malicious Roncalli-anecdotes would back up this theory: at the pope's audience on December 29, 1944 with the newly appointed nuncio, who was making a stopover in Rome on the flight from Ankara to Paris, Pius XII began with the curt announcement that he had exactly seven minutes to spare. To which Roncalli replied, politely but firmly, "In that case the remaining six minutes are superfluous," and then left the room. Unfortunately, in all likelihood it's just a story.

Of course, there's also another way of reading the facts. The pope may have quite deliberately sought out Roncalli from the field of candidates because of his irreplaceable talents. The French chargé d'affaires, Hubert Guérine, learned from one curial functionary that the pope chose Roncalli "on account of his experience and his big heart." The man from Istanbul had two things going for him: his "clean slate"—in the Balkans neither the local churches nor the Vatican had collaborated with totalitarian regimes—and his sympathy for a Christian democracy, which he had shown in Bergamo and which had looked so suspicious back then.

If those were really the pope's motives, then it was probably his "minister of the interior," Montini, who put him on Roncalli's track. There no longer was a cardinal secretary of state: the mistrustful Pius XII handled this office himself (just as the seventy-five-year-old German federal chancellor, Konrad Adenauer, also took over the foreign ministry). Power in the Vatican was divided now between Monsignor Tardini, as "secretary for the Extraordinary Affairs of the Holy See" and Roncalli's old friend, Deputy Montini, who was in charge of the domestic life of the Church. Montini no doubt correctly thought that a good pastor could better deal with General de Gaulle and his inquisitors than a cool diplomat.

As a matter of fact, the unknown Nuncio Roncalli, the man with no political baggage, did succeed, with a great deal of skill and his enormous human gifts, in putting relations between church and state (or rather, secular society) in France on a new footing. True, every now and then a Parisian mob gathered and pelted priests with stones; but the atmosphere of cultural warfare eased up. In the end only three bishops were replaced; and old Archbishop Saliège of Toulouse, who had himself carried into his cathedral on a stretcher to preach against the deportations of the Jews, was made a cardinal, and the nation felt pride and joy.

Needless to say, it's no longer possible to report in detail about Roncalli's share in defusing the conflict. He did cleverly drag out the procedure by asking for the original documents on the transgressions of the unpatriotic bishops and by having the material scrutinized in Rome; but the Parisian government also showed itself increasingly open to compromise. When de Gaulle succeeded in pushing through the appointment of philosopher Jacques Maritain, a Catholic but an independent one, as ambassador to the Holy See, the ice rapidly began to melt. The Vatican bureaucracy, we are told, once again bypassed the nuncio and, at times, dealt directly with Paris. That may be, but without Roncalli the wounds and calcification would never have healed so quickly; and the new atmosphere of open dialogue would have been much longer in coming.

Roncalli showed tact and sensitivity as soon as he arrived in Paris, when he wrote a "modest letter" to all French bishops and introduced himself as a *confrère* who was ready and willing to learn. He took part in a moving liturgy beneath the Eiffel Tower to celebrate the return of prisoners of war and concentration camp survivors. "Around a hundred priests in prisoners' uniforms distributed holy communion," the nuncio reported to a colleague. "In this way we move between the tragic visions of suffering and death and reawakening life."

During these same years the German POWs in Block 6 of the Le Courday camp near Chartres got to know the spontaneous, unconditionally credible humanity with which as pope Roncalli would later entrance the entire world. He wasn't satisfied with a routine scheduled visit; he kept coming back, spied into all corners, sat down by the sickbeds.

"The stocky man, with Italian nimbleness," a camp inmate recalls,

spread a strange atmosphere of confidence, cheerfulness, clowning cordiality, and palpable compassion. Outgoing to the point of self-forgetfulness, he seemed like the lovable opposite of an angular ascetic, although his natural piety moved everyone; and so he was the right man for people like us, who were nailed down and, in a odd sort of way, yearning. . . . Nobody and nothing could hold Nuncio Roncalli back from celebrating the holy sacrifice of the mass with the camp inmates, from distributing communion himself, and from sitting down with the men afterwards in the dining hall (a rather drafty place with wooden tables and benches) and seeing whether they liked the food. And no one (least of all his escort of colonels and majors) could stop him from looking into all corners of the gigantic dormitory (code name: stalactite cave), which was bitterly cold in winter and from showing the gentlemen accompanying him by his sad and emphatic expression what he thought of the whole thing. Then his eye ran up the triple-decker bunk beds; and as soon as he saw a prisoner stationed in front of the bed, he tipped his round hat a little. That message too was clear.

It goes without saying that Nuncio Roncalli liked to visit the "seminary behind barbed wire" that had been set up in Le Coudray for POWs who were students of theology (at times it held as many as 400 candidates). Under pitiable conditions, but with burning zeal, they studied Bible, church history, and preaching techniques. Roncalli ate with the young theologians out of their mess tins, asked how they were getting along, arranged to get them books and coal, and became friends with the legendary Abbé Franz Stock, who was pastor to the German Catholic community in Paris during the war, who accompanied almost 2,000 condemned French Resistance fighters to their place of execution, and who, now a prisoner himself, became a pioneer of German-French reconciliation.

On Good Saturday, 1947 he ordained two theology students from the diocese of Rottenburg to the priesthood.

Since he could hardly speak a word of German, the nuncio conversed with the POWs in broken Latin, which after several years at the front the students couldn't speak very fluently either. Roncalli would break out into his cheerful, never wounding laugh and describe how hard it had been for him, a peasant boy, to learn Latin.

Behind the scenes the nuncio, along with the French bishops, made every effort to shorten their prison time and enable the POWs, who still numbered 260,000, to return home. When the last ones managed to leave for Germany, French railroad workers suddenly went on strike. The return train was stuck on a siding for seven days. The nuncio organized the delivery of several truckloads of food with lightning speed.

Granted, Roncalli had no diplomatic training, but he thought in the context of history. He understood very well that the separation of church and state, like the basically secular bias of public life in France, had a long tradition behind it (as far back as 1904 the government had abrogated the concordat signed by Napoleon and the pope). His experiences in Turkey were helpful to him on this score. Here, too, in France something positive could obviously be gained from the distance that the state kept between itself and religion: many Catholics wouldn't like to give up the freedom and independence they had gained by it.

Of course, they suffered when the state praised their outstanding schools (twenty-two percent of all French students went to the *écoles libres*, most of which were Catholic), but made ridiculously small contributions to support them. In the debate over the new constitution Socialists and Communists even called for ending all subsidies, maliciously pointing to the inglorious role played by many church leaders during the occupation.

Once again Roncalli tried to pour oil on the waters. He paid his respects to France's secular culture: "Apart from the fear of God's name," much had been achieved here, "that basically constitutes the substance of civilization." And thus in passing he alluded discreetly, without trumpeting, to the quality of the Catholic educational institutions.

Nuncio Roncalli traveled back and forth across France, from Brittany to Corsica; he visited pilgrimage shrines and congregations of nuns; he was the guest of the fishermen of the *Sables d'Olonne* and the winegrowers of Beaune. He invited everyone to breakfast, made new friends every day, and had no fear rubbing shoulders with anyone. At the Arc de Triomphe there was an annual celebration of the storming of the Bastille, which had inaugurated the French Revolution in 1789. At one such memorial there was a torrential downpour, whereupon Roncalli unselfconsciously slipped his arm through the Soviet ambassador's, huddled beneath the man's capacious umbrella, and engaged him in animated conversation. He regularly invited workers who were fixing something in the nuncio's residence to share a glass of wine with him. For some time an Italian welder named Giuseppe is said to have dined at the nuncio's every first Saturday of the month—along with his wife and seven children.

Roncalli's ability to charm people was unquestioned, even then. "He is the only man in Paris in whose company you have the physical sensation of peace," said foreign minister and later president of the European parliament, Robert Schuman. Schuman was a devout Catholic, and his name has even been added lately to the list of candidates for beatification. But liberals as well were carried away by nuncio's hearty warmth, moved by the sensitivity that he brought to the cares and problems of his conversation partners, and fascinated by the transparency of his person.

In 1950 some theology students from Poitiers got in a car crash while in Italy, and were taken to a hospital in Ravenna. Shortly afterwards Roncalli arrived home on vacation in Sotto il Monte. Two days later he was at the bedside of the injured seminarians in Ravenna.

On the other hand, his public appearances met with a mixed reception. Roncalli's political deftness, his eye for new trends in French Catholicism, his difficult role in the web of interests involving the "home office" in Rome, the French national Church, Parisian politics, and the largely unbelieving mainstream of French society, were rated very differently by his companions, opponents, and critical observers. On the Parisian diplomatic scene, naturally enough, expectations ran higher, and there were far more opportunities to make a fool of oneself than in Sofia and Ankara. At any rate, in its studies of the life and work of Pope Roncalli the *Istituto per le Scienze Religiose* in Bologna has unearthed some rather ambivalent estimates of his activities in Paris. His appearances stirred up a "mixture of amusement and irritation." People mocked him for the rambling style of his talks, which were seasoned with occasionally "silly" jokes, and his weakness for good food. Some rather nasty fellow Catholics from the *Mouvement Républicain Populaire*, the party of Christian Democrats, had even nicknamed him *pulcinella*, meaning a buffoon or, in a political context, a lackey or spy of the Roman curia with no convictions of his own.

The fact that some of his talks came to grief was probably due, in the first instance, to the fact that Roncalli's French wasn't the best. And then he always had a predilection for flowery phrases. "In a few days the door of your house will be festooned with a fresh crown of orange blossoms," he burbled in his second New Year's address to General de Gaulle, before the assembled *Corps diplomatique*—instead of just congratulating him on his daughter's up-and-coming marriage.

"His natural good humor and his love of familiar *bons mots* (a whole collection could be cited) don't always inspire respect," Father Rouquette cautiously notes.

> Also, in his speeches he continually spoke about trivial things; that way he avoided taking a position. The result was that his listeners expressed their amusement with a lack of respect that bordered on an uproar. . . . At the congress of the *Union des Oeuvres* in Nancy, which dealt with burning pastoral issues, he spoke to us in the marvelous *palais* on Stanislas Place, going on forever about a pilgrimage he had just made to the places where St. Benedict Joseph Labre used to live—to the astonishment of several thousand priests in attendance. One of them, who was sitting next to me, said: 'So that's a nuncio?' Another time, in the course of a great ceremony in Rheims, he spoke mainly about wine and wine barrels, as the whole auditorium echoed with laughter.

A naïve bon vivant, whom no one took very seriously—or so it might seem, if one read such reports in isolation. The many massively self-critical passages in his diary further strengthen this negative image: "My talkativeness often misleads me into exaggerations," Roncalli confesses during a retreat in Holy Week, 1945. "Careful, careful: I have to be able to keep silent and learn how to speak with measure." Then follows, of course, the real motive for such self-laceration—not the fear of making a fool of himself, but the reluctance to harm others. "I have to be able to restrain myself (and to actually do that) from judging persons and ideas . . . I have to be specially attentive to make love of neighbor live. That is my rule."

Roncalli's indestructible sense of humor saw to it that his weaknesses and mistakes didn't do much damage. Once when he wanted to preach in French at St. Pierre de Chaillot, the microphone went dead, and instead of the nuncio, the only thing to be heard was a deafening stream of howls and squeaks. Roncalli left the pulpit, took up a position in the nave, and spoke audibly enough without technical assistance: "Dear children, you didn't hear what I said. But that makes no difference; it wasn't interesting. And I don't speak French especially well. My dear departed old mother, who was a peasant, didn't start me studying it early enough."

He preferred making fun of his own ample girth before others did. After a ceremony at the Académie Française, he announced that he had a wonderful seat. "One hears such exalted things! Unfortunately, the chairs have room for only half a nuncio." President Édouard Herriot, who was both a radical socialist and one of Roncalli's good friends, thoughtfully asked him whether people improved with age, "That depends," the nuncio replied. "It's like wine: time makes some kinds better." A rather tasteless interlocutor once tried to embarrass him, and said he must feel awkward at dinners where the women went around in generous décolleté. "No," Roncalli answered serenely, "whenever a woman wears a dress that's too revealing, people don't look at her, but at the apostolic nuncio!"

The kindly old gentleman in the purple of an archbishop could also be mordant and sarcastic, and above all quick on the draw when someone wanted to injure or exploit him. De Gaulle's brother Pierre, who was mayor of Paris at the time, thought he was bound to interpret the presence of the nuncio at a municipal reception as a sort of papal blessing on the just-founded Gaullist party—and said so. There was an embarrassed silence. In his reply the nuncio chatted with his usual liveliness about his visit to the international book fair and said: "I was particularly glad to discover that among the oldest books published in France was one by a compatriot of mine from Bergamo, a 16th century humanist named Gasparino de Barsizzi." He glanced briefly over to Pierre de Gaulle, then turned to the gathering, and added with an amiable smile: "The book is about good manners."

There is yet another story about a banquet in Paris, at which another gauche jester handed around a picture of a naked woman to test the reaction of the poor celibate. Roncalli looked at the photo and as he passed it back to its grinning owner, asked: "Your wife, I assume?"

People liked Roncalli because even in the feudal environment of the nunciature he remained simple and modest. In Paris Roncalli had two male secretaries and three nuns who worked as domestics. He traveled around France in a black Cadillac. But in his neighborhood he was recognized as the corpulent, ever-amiable abbé, who strolled through the streets or chatted with Yvette Morin at the newspaper kiosk on the Avenue Marceau (Morin was a Jew whose mother had been a prisoner in the women's concentration camp at Ravensbrück)—or enthusiastically browsed through the stalls of the *bouqinistes* on the banks of the Seine, looking for antiquarian treasures. Pius XII is said to have indignantly scolded him for this, insisting that such rambles hurt the nuncio's dignity.

But meanwhile criticism from Rome was just part of the little everyday annoyances that Angelo Roncalli could calmly brush aside. "You see, my dear Anna," he wrote to his niece in Advent, 1946, "a few days ago I entered my 66th year; and if I don't look in the mirror, I can fool myself, I still feel so young. But for a long time I've gotten used to thinking of heaven every day. That way all the allurements of the world fade away." Yes, here in the nunciature he dealt with princes, statesmen, and scholars; but, "Nothing disconcerts me anymore. I think about the simplicity of our life in the Colombera; and nothing fills me with so much enthusiasm as the thought of gently and humbly doing my job . . ."

In order to be able to counter the usual collections of anecdotes about "good Pope John" with the most faithful, warts-and-all portrait possible, the scholars in Bologna went through all of Roncalli's writings—from the first diary entries of the fourteen year-old seminarian to the notes jotted down on the last day of his life—and came out with a computerized concordance of all the terms and themes in them.

People had long since known, at least in Paris, that the Lombard peasant's son, with his rather homespun piety, had problems adjusting to the enlightened, urban Catholicism of France, and that his relations with the "worker priests" were ambiguous. It was no news either how harshly he had judged Teilhard de Chardin, the brilliant prophet of a "cosmic Christ." Nuncio Roncalli: "That Teilhard . . . !

Breaking through encrusted habit, John XXIII liked to walk through the streets of Rome. Here in 1962 he is on the way to the Capranica Theological College. A popular joke turned "the transitional pope" (*papa di passaggio*) into "the pople in transit" (*papa di passeggio*).
Courtesy UPI

Can't he be satisfied with teaching the catechism and the social doctrines of the Church, instead of dishing up all these problems?"

But until the publications from Bologna no one had known what people in Parisian governmental circles thought about the nuncio. For one thing, there was resentment against his obvious lack of interest in contacts with the *Quai d'Orsay*, the Foreign Ministry. During his entire eight-year time in office, the complaint ran, only once did he ever send a note to the authorities; and he had shown up there only, so to speak, when summoned. He didn't even inform the ministry about his frequent travels through the country, as had been the custom.

In the Ministry of the Interior again it was the head of the cultural division, the Protestant François Méjan, who in 1949 vented his wrath to the Quai d'Orsay: "Contrary to the practice followed by his predecessors ever since 1921, the apostolic nuncio apparently wishes to preside at all important religious festivities that take place in our country." And in a retrospect dated 1955: "Practically speaking, the nuncio tried to become the actual head of the Church in France."

Of course, there were also observers who viewed Roncalli's many appearances in the provinces and his seemingly indiscriminate contacts with all political camps as a sign that this passionate pastoral caregiver pretending to be a diplomat really wanted to get an authentic feel and love for this foreign country.

Faced with such reproaches, Roncalli reacted in his usual disarming fashion. It was quite right, he confessed to chief of protocol Dumaine, that at the beginning of the century Cardinal Ferrata had gone to the ministry every week. "But back then the foreign ministers were generally opponents of the Church, and the nuncio had to make himself noticed. However, that's not the case with me; because I'm among friends, and under no circumstances do I want to expose them!"

On the other hand, Christian democrats with good connections to the Church, chided the artless Italian for befriending Socialists and radicals. He had, after all, actually given Vincent Auriol, the president of the Republic and a leftist figurehead, a copy of Guareschi's *Don Camillo and Peppone*. Strangely enough, at the very same time an advisor of the foreign ministry was complaining about Roncalli's good relations with right-wingers.

In general, the French held it against the nuncio for being, at first, so astonishingly uninformed about the French educational system: He had wondered out loud that here there were public and private schools side by side, whereas Italy got by with public schools. He had completely overlooked the fact that the public school system in Italy was sectarian. Unless appearances are deceiving, his superiors in Rome were equally dissatisfied with Roncalli. De Gaulle's ambassador to the Vatican, Jacques Maritain, sent word to Paris on February 12, 1947 that Monsignor Tardini had said laudatory things about the information he was getting from the nunciature; but "on the other hand he did not conceal his rather low estimation of Monsignor Roncalli's qualities as a diplomat."

Maritain's successor noted that the nuncio was criticized for "slowness" and lack of interest in paperwork. Several visitors were surprised to find Roncalli sitting in front of a completely empty desk. His true friend Montini, to be sure, the companion and antagonist of the skeptical Tardini in the Vatican Secretariat of State, was happy to tell the French ambassador that, yes, the nuncio had objected to a series of candidates for bishop favored by Rome (which also says something about Roncalli's independent judgment and frankness). But, with his suggestions and evaluations, Roncalli had seen to it that the "strategic points" were filled by "notable prelates."

But then again the representatives of the government thought differently, at least in the conflict-ridden period immediately after the war. The nuncio's office, they said, used to present candidates "whose mediocrity guaranteed their total obedience to the Holy See," as one official from the Quai d'Orsay pointedly remarked in November 1945.

It's difficult today to put together a conclusive picture from such contradictory testimony. The same Georges Bidault, who came from the Catholic youth movement, who led the uprising in Paris against the German occupiers, and later became foreign minister, who disdained Roncalli as a "fat man stuffed with soup," also called him a "flexible and good negotiator."

Maybe the politicians in Paris underestimated him the same way the ecclesiastical diplomats in the Vatican had done before. Often enough Roncalli's jests and kind words concealed a sharp insight that he cleverly kept to himself and hid away beneath harmless chatter. In any case Father Rouquette, who has already been quoted several times, was not deceived: when you visited the nuncio, he kept telling stories; he showed you coffee table books of his beloved *paese* of Bergamo or presented you with tomes on church history bought from Parisian antiquaries. But all that was "only to prevent discussion of serious subjects."

Historian Henri Daniel-Rops offered this sober, but balanced judgment:

> Msgr. Roncalli had won the reputation of a man who was always talking, always moving, who listened badly to his conversation-partners, and who entertained his listeners with a thousand arguments totally irrelevant to the subject everyone was waiting to discuss. He himself laughed at his droll notions and had a disturbing tendency to make witty remarks. But to stop short at these observations would be to misunderstand him. As a matter of fact, if one paid close attention to his—undoubtedly deliberate—verbal torrent, one could from time to time make out a little sentence, generally an elliptical and allusive one, in which he suddenly revealed a profound thought. And the man whom sophisticates took to be a distracted chatterer, was perfectly capable of repeating, six months later, a line that someone had directed at him and that he had apparently not even been listening to.

Cardinal Maurice Feltin, who had become archbishop of Paris in 1949, spoke in a similar vein. Feltin was, like Roncalli, a peasant's son from a mountain village in the foothills of the Alps and, again like Roncalli, a passionate pastoral caregiver and a firm opponent of the nuclear arms race. After Roncalli's election as pope, Feltin told French journalists that the nuncio had always been amiable and always tried to smooth out differences; "but when the situation called for action, he didn't lack determination. His goodness wasn't mushy; it was powerful. And meanwhile he's clever, sharp-eyed, far-sighted. He doesn't let himself be influenced by either one side or the other, and I could cite a few examples to prove that."

Roncalli's wanderlust often ran into criticism. The nuncio particularly liked to head for the open road whenever unpleasant mail was expected from Rome. But nowadays some historians see this as a positive feature of the way he handled his office: "Roncalli, who felt uncomfortable in the tight-fitting clothes of the ambassador," writes Professor Fouilloux of Lyon, "practices a non-conformist diplomacy, preferably with personal, occasionally daring, connections." In contrast to his stiff, cerebral predecessor, Nuncio Valeri, he wanted to a be "a priest of flesh and blood."

Had he been a naïve Parsifal, Angelo Roncalli would hardly have passed the trenchant judgments about his environment that he did when, in 1948 during his annual retreat with the Benedictines of Calcat, he wrote in his diary:

> What a wretched figure all the intellectuals of the century cut, all the smart-alecks and sharpies of this earth, including some Vatican diplomats, when placed in the light of the frankness and purity that radiates from this fundamental and great teaching of Jesus and his saints!

Whenever otherwise "competent clerics," practiced any form of "mistrust or impoliteness, toward whomever, above all toward the little ones, the poor and the insignificant," it wounded him deeply. But then he preferred silence, because that was a better educational method than harsh action.

"My windows are wide open," he once said to a diplomat, "and my ears are ready and waiting to listen; but on many topics my lips are sealed."

In 1951 Nuncio Roncalli was appointed the first permanent Vatican observer at UNESCO, which had been established in Paris. In two far-reaching addresses, which he gave then before the General Assembly and a year later at a conference, he sketched out a convincing program for trustful cooperation between Catholics and non-Catholics that anticipated the changes in direction by the later Council. In contrast to most of the curial bureaucrats, Roncalli saw this sort of international umbrella organization with educational and cultural interests not as competition for the Church, but as a possible partner. UNESCO should be a "lofty school of mutual respect," without losing sight of the religious and cultural values of the individual nations. He quoted one of his predecessors, who in 1883 had formulated the motto in the Élysée palace: "To look into one another's eyes without mistrust, to approach one another without fear, to help one another, without losing face!"

Actually, he said, Catholics should always live in this sort of atmosphere, enriched by a faith that united the best values of human culture, but full of respect and love for all those made in the image and likeness of God. History was there "to be mastered and led toward salvation, not toward the shipwreck of the world." Sometimes the impression can arise, Roncalli cautiously suggested, that pedagogical, cultural, and scholarly work was lacking in vital energy and self-worth. Then Catholics should impart to it through the wisdom, the power, and the pungency of the Sermon on the Mount, "the salt that guarantees the permanence and the exquisite goodness of success."

And the nuncio showed himself to be not at all naïve in the conflict over Algeria. That country was still a French colony at the time. In the Second World War the Resistance had entrenched itself in Algeria, but the Muslim population made increasingly strong demands for their freedom. In 1954 when the military revolt against France began under Ben Bella that would lead eight years later to independence, Roncalli was no longer nuncio. But he had experienced in all its intensity the bitter struggle between the supporters of the freedom movement and the adherents of the old colonial system.

In his New Year's addresses before the diplomatic corps he combined clever politeness and prophetic partisanship for the oppressed, whose situation he had come to know on a 6,000 mile journey through North Africa. On December 30, 1948, speaking to President Auriol he pointedly called freedom a "daughter of God" and an inalienable human right. He also celebrated, in a quite general but unmistakable fashion, the "noble determination" of those statesmen "who prefer justice and brotherhood between the nations to even the most justified special interests. On December 30, 1950 he warned about solving problems with violence. War, he said, meant "the destruction of culture and the return to barbarism."

The crucial question that causes enormous headaches for the Roncalli scholars is about the continuity and possible breaks in the personal development of the man who would later be pope. Did a conformist Vatican functionary, nervously eyeing his superiors, a man with a narrow intellectual horizon and unpretentious piety, suddenly become transformed, as if by the eruption of an inner volcano, into the revolutionary on the chair of St. Peter? Or was the rebellious John XXIII already present in pastor-diplomat Roncalli, whose goodness and affability from the very beginning knew neither bounds nor taboos? Was he a friendly provocateur, who should have called himself Peter, the rock, because he could thwart both the deliberate counter-arguments of timid co-workers and the solid inertia of battle-tested curial cardinals with a broad smile and one or two resolute sentences?

Shortly after the death of Pope John, the archbishop of Bologna Cardinal Giacomo Lercaro, who knew Roncalli very well and shared his goals, as one of the charismatic guiding figures of the Council, published a book about him. *Giovannni XXIII—Linee per una ricerca storica* has been all too neglected. In it Lercaro warns against imagining a grand rupture in Roncalli's personality. He wasn't a simple person whose uncomplicated straightforwardness ("lacking any advanced preparation in knowledge and experience") transformed him at a certain moment into "a submissive instrument of the Holy Spirit, capable of making a few elementary decisions perfectly in keeping with what was called for, without actually being aware of it, without making any contribution of his own." Roncalli's life, Lercaro writes, was no "joke on God's part"; and no new person came into being when at the end of a long career he was elected pope and "mediocrity gave birth to genius."

That was because at the moment of the conclave, in the fall of 1958, the man raised to the papacy already had at his disposal an extraordinary wealth of knowledge and experience. "This wasn't something he received as a gift," Lercaro makes clear. "He acquired it through patience and perseverance." Roncalli had gotten an unusual education, "not especially broad, but deep, not outwardly brilliant, but distinguished by its soundness, balance, clarity, and power to synthesize." It wasn't a merely bookish education, but a vital and creative one. Lercaro calls Roncalli a "man of the sources," not of scholastic knowledge and scholarly analysis. This lifelong, persevering confrontation with the sources of Christian spirituality was bound up with Roncalli's realism, his sense for the concrete, his loving observation of the ever-changing world around him.

Both the case-hardened spokesmen for scholasticism as well as the self-confident modern questioners were bound to misjudge this sort of education, Lercaro maintains. "To the former it seemed naïve, because it wasn't expressed in the tried and tested formulas of scholasticism or curial practice, and because its consequences tended to overthrow all their systems. To the latter it seemed mediocre, as a lack of information and critical intelligence, because every sort of intellectual complexity was alien to it. But to both sides it appeared to be a rather facile and unchecked good-naturedness . . .

The "leap" shortly before the end of his life, misunderstood as a break in identity, was probably also a perfectly natural result of the freedom acquired with his new position. All the way into his eighth decade Angelo Roncalli had groaned beneath the weight of his superiors—all those teachers, seminary rectors, bishops, and curial officials. A pope, of course, no longer has any earthly chief over him. He can do whatever his heavenly Lord emboldens him to.

"We didn't understand at the time," Robert Rouquette, admitted after the pope's death. "When he was in Paris, we thought he was inclined to fundamentalism"—in other words, to a ghetto mentality and the rejection of any opening to "secular" trends. Should people have guessed "that the nuncio's external conformism cloaked a repressed intellectual freedom, which was waiting for the moment when it could reveal itself?"

Probably no one could have guessed. The rapid intellectual currents surging through French Catholicism in those days seemed to remain alien to the portly nuncio, who kept on talking about Bergamo and felt particularly at home at folksy pilgrimage sites. We don't know if he ever read Claudel, Mauriac, Bernanos, or Julien Green, whether he heard the challenge of Sartre's desperate existentialism or the wild revolt of Albert Camus against a God without pity.

One thing is certain: Given his overall outlook and his painful experiences with headquarters in Rome, the nuncio did not think of himself simply as a watchdog or spy. On the other hand, obedience was one of the virtues that he especially strove for. He would never have dreamed of calling into question the role of the papacy, which guaranteed the Church's connection to its roots. And the many curial politicians, guardians of the faith and censors in the Vatican, little as he may have liked some of them, all belonged, in one way or another, to that Petrine office.

Hence it was altogether logical that in 1947, during his retreat at a Jesuit residence in Paris, Nuncio Roncalli called himself to order: "Merely out of a wish to be obliging or the fear of causing scandal, I may not overlook the shortcomings or disguise the real situation with regard to religious life, the unsolved problems with the schools, the shortage of priests, or the spread of secularization and communism here in the eldest daughter of the Church."

Can the Roncalli phenomenon be deciphered by analyzing cases where despite all his conciliatory tendencies he was inevitably caught between the crossfire? In several perceptive pastoral letters the cardinal of Paris, Emmanuel Suhard, had called France a mission country and prescribed a radical cure for a Church that had gotten lazy. If it wished to enter into dialogue again with the intellectuals, the workers, and young women, it had to change its whole appearance and discover entirely new forms of pastoral care. Although Suhard was burdened by the charge of collaboration in the Pétain era, he had a razor-sharp mind and far-sighted awareness of contemporary problems. He didn't exactly endear himself to Rome by such daring solo flights.

In the four and a half years up till his death in 1949 the nuncio met Suhard at least forty-five times. At first they were rather reserved with one another. Suhard, Father Rouquette maintains, feared the nuncio, and after such encounters he seemed "dark and unhappy." But an honest mutual appreciation soon sprang up. Roncalli began to learn from Suhard. He grasped the limits, but also the possibilities, of a church that had enormously strong roots in the country's culture and history, but that was threatening to become irrelevant to present-day social life. Jean Vinatier, who wrote a great biography of the cardinal, concludes that after his election as pope Roncalli proved to be a genuine *Suhardien*, a bold visionary in Suhard's steps.

As a matter of fact, the nuncio managed, working through his Roman confidant Montini, to launch an article in *L'Osservatore Romano* praising Suhard and his Mission de Paris, where unconventional pastoral methods were being tried out in a metropolitan milieu estranged from the Church. He obtained the Vatican's permission to dispense the sacraments in French—a daring innovation at the time—and to get legal recognition for a training center for the Mission de France that had been set up in Lisieux, although conservatives had been bombarding Rome with complaints against such a "proletarianization" of the clergy.

And here we have the specter that was causing such fear and horror among bourgeois Catholics in France, but still more among observers far off in Rome: the "worker priests." In Lisieux young priests were being specially trained to serve in the workplace. In industrial regions of France, teams of priests—about 120 men in all—took full-time, long-term jobs in factories in order to be close to their friends on the assembly line or the shop floor. In their wretched apartments they celebrated mass with their neighbors and coworkers, took part in strikes, were busy in union activities. Needless to say, such priests could no longer be easily supervised by the church hierarchy. They had a certain economic independence, and often enough they marched behind the red flag of communism. Monsignor Ottaviani at the Holy Office in Rome wanted to know whether they regularly said their breviary and kept their vow of celibacy.

Suhard had already approved the experiment back in 1943; at the time it mostly involved priests who had signed up to go to Germany, where a great number of French workers were slaving

away in arms factories. Once again it's impossible to make out exactly what Nuncio Roncalli thought about the "worker priests," since
the correspondence between the nuncio's office and the Vatican is
still under lock and key. In 1956, at any rate, as an Italian cardinal
he delivered a speech to Catholic lay activists and told a tear-jerk-
ing story that the opponents of the experiment kept bringing up:
the comrades of one worker priest had begged him to quit his factory job so he could devote himself completely to the pastoral care
of their wives and children.

The claim has been made that while he was nuncio, Roncalli wan-
gled from Rome a preliminary permission for the worker priests.
When the Vatican made cutbacks—limiting factory work to three
hours a day, no political involvement whatsoever, mandatory participation in "normal" parish life—Roncalli was no longer in Paris. But
the definitive ban on the experiment in 1959 came during his own
papacy; and he wrote Cardinal Feltin a Solomonic letter, declaring
that the "sacred character" of the priesthood had to be preserved
"under all circumstances," which didn't exclude the possibility of
"going out to the workers and bringing them the breath of light and
grace." In 1964 his successor Paul VI, the former Monsignor
Montini, again gave permission for a diluted form of the plan.

We also don't know whether and to what extent Roncalli was
called in by the *Sanctum Officium*, the Vatican authorities in matters
of faith, or by the pope himself, when sanctions were issued against
French theologians. In 1950 the encyclical *Humani generis*
appeared, a thunderbolt aimed at the whole *théologie nouvelle*; and in
the period that followed its most brilliant representatives lost their
teaching positions: the Dominican Yves Congar, who thought of the
Church as the people of God (not as a hierarchical pyramid) and
opposed its disunity with a vision of a resolute ecumene; the Jesuit
Henri de Lubac, who tried to organically link divine and human
nature; the Dominican Marie-Dominique Chenu, who with his theology of work restored dignity to the everyday lives of ordinary people and saw the Holy Spirit at work in secular history.

When the encyclical was published, the nuncio once again

hastily took off. No statements from his office have been preserved. But he later appointed the exiled theologians as advisors to the Council, and their ideas marked his most important papal addresses. De Lubac would enjoy a particularly splendid rehabilitation in 1983 when John Paul II made him a cardinal.

So was Nuncio Roncalli a committed companion along the road to a spiritual revolution, or did he slam on the brakes at the bidding of a mistrustful church bureaucracy? Was he a joyful pioneer or a nervous onlooker? "God demands that we be clever; he doesn't demand that we be prophets." He liked to quote that remark of Pope Benedict XV, and he kept his cards close to his vest.

But it was the French ambassador to the Holy See, who as far back as 1954, four years before the death of Pius XII and a year after Roncalli's departure from Paris as nuncio, who signaled his government: "His Eminence Roncalli," wrote Vladimir d'Ormesson, had "very good prospects," come the next papal election.

I would only like to say that his tact and the incomparable combination of qualities which brought him success in Parisian circles, whether friendly or hostile to the Holy See, offer the same advantages that might one day make it possible for him to win the votes of the College of Cardinals. A comfortable choice for the strict conservatives and a reassuring one for the undecided or moderates, he may well emerge as the candidate of the 'middle.' In addition, I hear from various sources that his 'stock' is rising.

7

The Papacy

"I am Joseph, your brother.
—*Pope John XXIII*

IN NOVEMBER 1952 WORD CAME of his upcoming appointment as cardinal—a shock for the nuncio who had just turned seventy-one. True, his friend Montini had sent him a telegraph with the news that the Patriarch of Venice, Carlo Agostini, was on his deathbed; and they wanted to know whether Roncalli was prepared to be his successor. But who could guess what crazy ideas the Romans would come up with this time? Did they want to drag him off to the curia in his old age and leave him stagnating there at some Baroque desk? Maybe they would make him prefect for the Congregation of the Eastern-rite Churches, a subject that he really knew a lot about.

Archbishop Feltin found him "dispirited and sad," when he came to congratulate him—-the Vatican's intentions had, of course, already leaked out. "I'm not at all happy," the nuncio grumbled. "I can't imagine being in Rome where I'll have to go to some kind of *congresso* every day and do a lot of management work. That means nothing to me, I'm a pastor." To top it all off, he had gotten, along with Montini's telegram, a letter from Sotto il Monte that his beloved sister Ancilla had cancer and wasn't given long to live.

One can only assume that he felt relief when shortly after Christmas he learned of the death of the Venetian Agostini. Soon after that came the confirmation that he was to be the new patriarch

1963: The Pope at one of his impromptu speeches on the street corners of Rome.

(as the bishops of Venice had been called since 1451), a post that offered an ideal combination of public appearances, responsible leadership, and pastoral care. For a passionate church historian like Roncalli, a specialist on the (sensitive) relationships between the Eastern and Western churches, Venice was a dream assignment.

Nevertheless, as he was leaving Paris, he wrote in some distress in his diary: "A separation full of pain, but gently comforted by the closeness to God and the agreeable knowledge that I got closer to people through kindness."

He commented with his usual calm on his elevation to cardinal, noting that the mighty purple robes had been worn by saints—and scoundrels. The much-desired cardinal's hat, he told his nephew Battista, would appear only at his funeral, when it would be carried behind the hearse. He had been informed that the patriarch had to live "as poor as a bird" in Venice, but the Lord would provide for him. On March 15, 1953 the new patriarch entered the city of lagoons with a splendid multi-colored flotilla of gondolas proceeding down the Grand Canal. His welcoming speech instantly won the hearts of the Venetians, "I would like to speak to you with the greatest candor," he began.

> You have been told things about me that greatly exaggerate my merits. Let me present myself in all humility. . . . I come from modest circumstances and I was brought up in contented and blessed poverty, a poverty that has few needs, that develops the noblest virtues and prepares you to soar high in life. Providence has removed me from my native village and sent me wandering over the streets of the world both east and west. It has brought me into contact with people of different religions and world views, with acute and threatening social problems, while preserving the peace and equilibrium I needed to explore and evaluate them. Holding fast to the unshakable basic principles of Catholic faith and morals, I have nonetheless been increasingly concerned more with what unites people than with what separates and opposes them.

"Now, at the end of a long life experience," Roncalli continued, "I come to Venice, the country and the sea that have been familiar to my ancestors for a good four hundred years . . . I have no news to bring you, as Marco Polo did when he returned to his people. . . . But I recommend to your good will a person, *che vuol essere semplicemente vostro fratello*, who simply wants to be your brother, lovable, accessible, full of understanding."

The Venetians were enthusiastic about him. Anyone could enter his sparsely furnished palazzo without a prior appointment or protocol formalities. He didn't want to have his own motorboat; he preferred to chat with the passengers on public transportation. "Come, sit here with me," he would encourage the people on the *vaporetto*. "You pay the same fare that I do. Come, let's have a little chat."

The patriarch could be seen at a café near St. Mark's Square, savoring a glass of vino bianco. You might meet him on the waterfront of the Grand Canal, resting on the stone stairs and conversing with the gondoliers. When his friend from Paris, Cardinal Feltin, came to visit him, Roncalli took him out on St. Mark's Square and asked the city band to play the *Marseillaise*. There was, people claimed, not one parish in the sprawling diocese of Venice where the patriarch had not celebrated mass at least once.

Were these bold gestures meant for reporters? When Roncalli met someone whose heart was heavy, he could take endless amounts of time for the person. Somehow he had heard that a young Venetian woman had fallen hopelessly in love with a French truck driver whom she met on the Lido during vacation. The Lothario had driven off without leaving an address behind, and the girl was sick with grief. The patriarch was so moved that he wrote to a Parisian acquaintance, a chaplain, and asked him to search for the truck driver, about whom he knew only that he had blond hair and blue eyes. The young man *was* tracked down, but unfortunately it turned out that he was already engaged to a French woman.

Shortly before Christmas Roncalli read in the newspaper that the wife of a leading member of Catholic Action in Venice had died. He spontaneously called up the widower, Eugenio Bacchion, and proposed, "This is your first Christmas with an empty place at your table. Would you like to come with your children to have Christmas dinner with me?"

Venice was and is no typical metropolis like Milan or Turin, but in the shipyards and steelworks of Porto Marghera or Mestre one finds the same problems as in other large industrial cities; and in the summer the immense crowds of tourists bring money but conflicts as well to the city of churches and palaces. In an open letter Roncalli asked the guests—-who weren't always sure of their style—-not to dress too scantily, "since Italy doesn't exactly lie on the equator," and there, too, one might meet lions in furs, and crocodiles in expensive scaly outfits. He took more seriously the cares of the financially weak, whose misery he saw behind the splendid face of the fairytale city. A few days after taking office he visited the factories of Marghera, where many young Venetians earned their bread, and celebrated a mass for the victims of workplace accidents. The following year he held the Easter liturgy with the workforce of AGIP, Italy's government-owned petroleum company, in the industrial harbor.

The patriarch knew what hard work was. He had gotten used to getting up at four o'clock in the morning, and he was often still at his desk at ten o'clock at night. As always, he traveled around everywhere. In the five years he spent in Venice thirty new parishes were founded, above all in industrial areas. Roncalli was a rather sturdy old man. When they restored the shining angel, visible from far and wide, atop the bell tower of San Marco, the patriarch bravely hiked up the narrow tower staircase to bless the heavenly messenger. Perched hundreds of feet in the air and balancing himself on a stone block, he leaned out of the campanile with his secretary Loris Capovilla clinging tightly to his cassock. When they had descended, people wondered why Capovilla's face was ashen.

Patriarch Roncalli hadn't lost his curiosity about people. He met with provincial counselors, fire fighters, religious superiors, art historians and nurses. He invited a rugby team and a soccer team from Porto Marghera to his official residence. He maintained good relations with Venice's Mayor Battista Giaquinto, even though the man was a Communist; and he encouraged the Christian Democrats to defend the interests of the little people. But he fought off all attempts to enlist him in the propaganda campaigns of the *Democrazia cristiana*. To their horror he made it clear at his inaugural visit to the town hall that he was in a house "that belongs to the people as a whole." The only person entitled to call himself or herself a Christian was someone working for a good cause. "That is why I am happy to be with you, although there may be some people here who don't call themselves Christians; still, on the basis of their good deeds they can be acknowledged as such. I give you all my fatherly blessing!"

In peasant villages and industrial parishes the division of labor between Don Camillo and Peppone could be carried out with a mixture of respect, good-humored teasing and continuous readiness to struggle. But on the higher levels of the Church and national politics strict distance was the order of the day, especially since the Italian Communists were still toeing the Stalinist line. The *Democrazia cristiana*, on the other hand, which had held a leading position in all governments since 1945, and which hitherto had been interested only in coalitions with its competitors on the right, could count on vigorous support from the pope and large portions of the clergy. Like all Italian bishops, Roncalli warned about "the impossibility of a marriage between the Christian and the Marxist views of social order." Like all representatives of the hierarchy, he admonished Catholics not to underestimate the dangers of socialism and secularism and to follow the pope. "This is a matter of discipline . . . All honor to freedom of thought, and personal convictions deserve respect—but within recognized limits."

But then he engaged in such scandalous solo actions as his greeting to the congress of the Socialist party of Italy, which met in Venice in 1957 under the leadership of Pietro Nenni. The meeting of the Reds, he said, certainly "had great significance for the development of our country," and it might contribute to bridging the gap between secular and Christian culture. *L'Unità*, the central organ of the Communist party, at once interpreted these friendly words as an offer to cooperate; and Monsignor Angelo dell'Acqua, who had taken Montini's place in the Vatican Secretariat of State after Montini was promoted to Milan as archbishop, issued an official reprimand. Roncalli also stubbornly refused to condemn the course of the Christian Democratic daily *Il Popolo del Veneto*, which just then was arguing for the opening of the party to the left, the *apertura a sinistra*, and a consistent agenda of social reforms. That was Montini's approach, but he no longer had much say in the Vatican; and the curial officials who set the tone exerted massive pressure on the bishops of the Veneto. For the sake of his beloved peace, Roncalli finally published a pastoral letter in which he rejected any *apertura a sinistra* if it was conducted "at all cost." The qualification was noted. He could not be moved to engage in repressions that went any farther.

The good-natured fool!—people in the Vatican groaned, failing to see that the presumably butter-soft patriarch was perfectly capable of taking vigorous action when he was convinced about a cause, "Hard as steel" was how his good friend from Verona, Bishop Urbani, who would be his successor in Venice, described him. Roncalli's emphatic protest prevented the city administration from moving the gambling casino from the Lido to the Palazzo Giustinian, in the center of Venice. And he forbade his clergy to buy TV sets—the mostly dreadful programs would keep priests from carrying out their pastoral duties. Speaking to the managers of the Biennale, the international art exhibit at the Lido, he recommended care in the presentation of avant-garde objects involving religion. But he was the first patriarch to visit the display, and he invited the artists to a reception. He didn't pretend to understand anything about abstract art, but joyfully noted that, "At least it doesn't conflict with either dogma or morality." He invited Igor Stravinsky to premiere his oratorio *Canticum sacrum in honorem Sancti Marci Evangelistae*, with its daring atonality and archaic rhythms, in San Marco, although the Vatican had voiced misgivings, because Stravinsky wasn't a Catholic.

Meantime the Romans had presumably given up trying to change the stubborn old priest with the magnetic charisma. Nonetheless he was consulted by three Vatican congregations: *Propaganda Fide*, Eastern-rite Churches, and Religious. He was allowed to continue his research and publish his study of Carlo Borromeo's visitation reports. Curial observers were relieved to note that the well-prepared diocesan synod of 1957 was staged in three days, without any controversial debates or rebellious resolutions.

But the address that he delivered about the "spiritual father-hood" of a bishop must have alarmed the mossbacks, whose sway in the Vatican after Montini's departure was absolute. "Authoritarian behavior stifles life," Roncalli said. "It mistakes harshness for strength and stiffness for dignity. Paternalism is a caricature of fatherliness. It considers people immature in order to safeguard its own superiority . . . it lacks respect for the rights of subordinates."

But in Rome they probably weren't reading the documents from Venice very closely; and the eighty-one-year-old pope Pius XII, who might have viewed such a program as a coded attack on his own administration, was too tired and too sick to take any interest in it.

The cardinal of Venice is traditionally one of the *papabili*, one of the possible candidates for pope. Giuseppe Sarto, later Pope Pius X, had been patriarch in Venice; and in the time after Roncalli Albino Luciani, too, was pope—John Paul I, the tragic "pope of 33 days." But that wasn't actually the reason why Cardinal Roncalli entered the conclave quite self-confidently when Pius XII died on October 9, 1958. The patriarch could figure that he had a rather realistic chance of being elected as a compromise candidate between the entrenched powers of the curia and the bishops of the major world cities who wanted the Church to change course.

That is just what he accomplished, which doesn't really fit into the generally accepted image of Angelo the simple son of a peasant. For example, on the day the conclave began Roncalli wrote openly to the bishop from his home, "Basically it doesn't matter whether the new pope comes from the province of Bergamo or not." He should send his nephew, Don Battista, to him, if he heard that the choice of the cardinals had fallen on Roncalli . . .

Of course, he couldn't very well close his ears to the gossip ema-nating from Rome, Venice, Bergamo, or Paris, and placing him front and center in the ranks of the serious *papabili*. When a pious muddle-headed character named Gaston Bardet published a book about his heavenly inspirations and prophesied the tiara for Roncalli, the candidate had had enough. "A couple of crazy Frenchmen," he burst out indignantly in a letter to his sister Maria,

> who have revelations and are clairvoyant, even told me the name that I'd take if I were elected pope. They're crazy, just crazy, one and all. Meanwhile I think about dying. I have a full load of work here . . . but I'm prepared and ready to die any day . . . You know, Maria, as a result of living this way in daily readiness for a good death, I maintain and strengthen in my heart, more than ever before, a still more vital and gentle peace that is a foretaste of heaven where our dear ones are waiting for us. Angelo was seventy-three when he wrote this letter.

Roncalli probably got the support of the influential French cardinals, who had fond memories of him from his time in Paris (even though, as we know, they sometimes misunderstood him). His Italian colleagues admired his foreign experience. In addition, his reputation for robust health had preceded him, even while he himself liked to joke about his age and often talked about death. Pius XII, who preferred doing without coworkers, had rarely named new cardinals; and so the College of Cardinals had not only shrunken, but also grown dreadfully gray: twenty-four of its fifty-one members were older than the seventy-six-year-old Roncalli. "In this ancient group," Peter Hebblethwaite notes in amusement, "some of the eighty-year-olds looked upon Roncalli as a sprightly youth." Then, too, after the harsh twenty-year rule of Pacelli, people wanted a successor who wouldn't govern for an eternity nor with an iron hand. Many wanted a phase of calm and reflection, time for a much needed, but thoughtful reorientation.

But the cardinals could hardly view candidate Roncalli as a mere emergency solution, a naïve, easily led old man. He wouldn't have concealed from them that he wanted a change of direction in the Vatican, as he had confessed to the director of the seminary in Venice after Pius's death: "We have to pray that his successor, whoever he may be, doesn't bring us a solution that only amounts to continuance, instead of the progress we need to match the eternal youth of the Church."

To be sure, in a man who radiated so much wisdom and down-to-earth kindness, such words had an entirely different ring. As someone who was sympathetic to the moderate progressives and didn't frighten the archconservatives, he was the ideal compromise candidate.

At fifty-three Archbishop Giuseppe Siri of Siena, confidant of the dead pope and spokesman for the traditionalists, was considered too young for the chair of St. Peter. For this reason the conservative fraction put curial cardinal Aloisi Masella into the running. He had made a name for himself in Brazil; and now, after the pope's death, as papal chamberlain he held the reins of the Vatican. But Masella was already seventy-nine and seemed worn out.

Many of the progressives, along with some especially clever journalists, were betting on the Armenian Gregory Peter Agagianian, an interesting figure with a full beard and an intellectual disposition. He was born in the Caucasus, but had come to Rome at age eleven to be educated. As a former patriarch of Cilicia, he gave off an aura of the Church Universal. At the same time, as the head of the *Propaganda Fide*, he could now be considered a genuine Roman. In the camp of the "moderns," the chances of the charismatic Archbishop Lercaro of Bologna were thought to be good, and among the conservatives people talked about Ruffini (Palermo) and Ottaviani (the curia). There was even some serious discussion of Montini, but it would have been a break with tradition to elect a non-cardinal.

Of course, one can only speculate about the course of the three-day conclave, and the detailed accounts some writers provide for each balloting have to be handled rather gingerly. This is especially true because initially there was a great deal of guessing, with no clear-cut heir apparent, as there was after John's death, when everybody was talking about Montini. In their desperation the newspapers offered as many as thirty-seven *papabili* with photos and résumés. But there are many indications that after the first "test votes" two blocs quickly formed: the conservative camp voted first for Masella and then for Siri, the benjamin among the cardinals, while the progressive wing favored the Armenian. Both camps blocked each other, until—we may suspect—the French broke the stalemate and presented Roncalli as a centrist acceptable to the majority. Or was the crucial contest, as other insiders claim, noting some obscure allusions by the pope himself, the race between Agaganian and Roncalli?

The Lombard peasant's son, with his combination of modesty and sovereign realism, would not have thought that he *had* to be pope, but it was clear that he *could* be. "A great fuss is being made over my poor self," he noted in his diary during the two weeks between the death of Pope Pius and the conclave. Some remarkable meetings took place, but, he maintained, they didn't shake his inner tranquility.

He was chosen in the eleventh or twelfth round of balloting, supposedly with thirty-eight of the fifty-one votes. In a noble gesture, he cast his own vote, as he himself later revealed, for Cardinal Valeri, his predecessor in the nunciature of Paris, a man who he thought at the time had been mistreated.

The election of a new pope in the Sistine Chapel, in full view of Michelangelo's "Last Judgment," with its angels and souls of the damned and a youthful Christ, is full of pregnant symbolic gestures. At the end of the conclave the canopies above the seats of the cardinals are drawn back, and only one remains open, over the seat of the chosen man. The dean of the College of Cardinals, the old, white-bearded Eugène Tisserant from France, an outstanding Orientalist and scholar, but also a former colonel who always put in a military appearance, marched slowly up to Roncalli and asked him whether he accepted the choice, and how he wanted to be called.

Roncalli's answer, amiable as its phrasing was, contained the first of the little rebellious upsurges for which he would be famous: "*Vocabor Johannes.* I will be called John." Not Pius XIII, not another Benedict or Leo. John had been his father's name, he began to explain quite innocuously, the name of the modest church where he had been baptized, and the name of the Lateran Basilica in Rome. Then he went on to explain: "It is the name that appears most frequently in the long line of Roman bishops. . . . quite apart from the question of legitimacy."

That was the crucial point, because by taking the name John,

Angelo Roncalli, with his fine historical education, abruptly thrust aside a man who had been a scandal in the list of the successors of St. Peter. There had already been a John XXIII. He was a Neapolitan nobleman named Baldassare Cossa, who made a career as a pirate and condottiere, and who bravely defended the Papal States against the assault by the King of Naples. In 1410 under massive pressure from the King of France he was elected pope (after murdering his predecessor, it is claimed). To his misfortune he let himself be talked into convoking a reform council in Constance, where the Council fathers found John's way of life so offensive that they deposed him in 1415. He spent a long time in prison, was consoled in 1419 by receiving the cardinal's hat, but died a few months afterwards. (The Bohemian rebel against Rome, Jan Hus, who had likewise been invited to Constance, had still worse luck: he was condemned by the Council and burned at the stake.)

To this day church historians disagree whether the pirate should be listed as an anti-pope (at the time there were two more claimants to the papacy, Gregory XII and Benedict XIII) or as a regularly elected office-holder. His tomb, sculpted by Donatello in the baptistery of Florence, bears the ambiguous inscription, "John, once the pope." If that is correct, then Roncalli would properly have to be called John XXIII, the Younger, as some experts actually demanded. In any event Roncalli had the courage to erase this blot on church history and bring the good biblical name of John back into honor.

The newly elected pope closed his address with the soothing assurance that almost all the popes named John had had a short reign, and he alluded to the fact that the Apostle John embodies in the Gospel the attitude of compassionate love: "Little children, love one another. Love one another, for that is the highest commandment of the Lord!"

As moved as Roncalli's colleagues were by this tender appeal, they were equally amazed by the self-confidence of their new head, whose voice never quavered as he read off this explanation from a prepared sheet. His next gesture was also a masterly one. The secretary of the conclave, Monsignor Alberto di Jorio, approached with the pope's white cap, the *zucchetto*. Roncalli took the new headgear and put his own red cardinal's cap, no longer needed, on the head of the nonplussed di Jorio. This was an ancient tradition and meant that the person distinguished in this way would be made a cardinal at the next opportunity (which in fact happened). But, for one thing, the most recent popes had not practiced the custom, and, for another, the monsignor had been a *persona non grata* to Pope Pius XII.

Thirty-six hours after his election, amid the hectic preparations for the coronation, making his way through the endless suites of rooms in the Vatican, and getting to know all his new coworkers, John found time to receive the Bavarian nun, Pasqualina Lehnert, and to make some reparations for the mean way she had been treated after Pope Pius's death. Sister Pasqualina had run the pope's household back in the time when he was still nuncio in Munich. He had taken her with him to Rome, and as rectory housekeepers will, she ran a very tight ship, jealously watching over her high-ranking protégé. She could strike fear even into the hearts of Vatican monsignori. In an allusion to the Litany of Loreto, she was maliciously called *virgo potens*, the powerful virgin.

The pope was barely dead when the pontifical household took its revenge. Sister Pasqualina was promptly shown the door, with two suitcases and the two beloved canaries of the dead pontiff as her only luggage. Articles appeared in the newspapers about the pope's German-dominated environment. John said not a word about this. He shook the old nun's hand, thanked her for the more than forty years of service at the Church's power center, and asked whether her future had been taken care of (she retired to the Swiss mother house of her order).

That's how he did things. Roncalli knew exactly what he wanted, and from the first day of his administration he worked out a clearly defined agenda in all his actions and statements, however spontaneous they might otherwise be. His plans included the Church's opening up to the questions of the "world," a cooperative style of leadership in the Church's governance, a humanization of the Holy See. That was the explanation behind his uncomplicated, kindly manner of dealing with people; and in this way he introduced a real revolution into the Apostolic Palace—while providing material for countless anecdotes.

For his "coronation" he invited almost forty brothers, sisters, nephews and nieces from Sotto il Monte, who were all terribly excited and wept with emotion when they were reunited with him. His sister Assunta had been at the bakery when the radio announced Roncalli's election. "My God, little Angelo!" she murmured in terror. However, he had already sent his nephew Don Battista back home at once, amiably enough but without hesitation: he didn't want to feed the faintest suspicion that being related to the pope could win anyone high office. That had happened in Pius's day, when various nephews were awarded lofty titles by the pope.

John was the first pope to deliver a sermon at his coronation, as if the five-hour ceremony weren't long enough for him. But perhaps he was trying to counter the triumphalism of the old rites, e.g., the formula with which the triple-decker tiara was placed on his head: "Know that you are the father of princes and kings, pope of the entire globe and Christ's deputy on earth!" In his speech Roncalli made it clear that he would disappoint everyone who looked on the pope as a statesman, a diplomat, a scholar or an "organizer of the coexistence of social forces." He simply wanted to be a good shepherd: "Other human qualities—education, clever diplomacy, organizational talent—may embellish and enrich a pontificate, but they cannot replace being a shepherd of the entire flock."

8

A Peasant's Shoulders and the Mystery of Roncalli

When I was a child I was called Angelo;
in the army, they ordered me around as Giuseppe,
and now I'm Giovanni.

—*Pope John XXIII*

ON THIS NOVEMBER 4TH he had to ascend the golden *sedia gestatoria*, which he didn't like, though it was no doubt a practical invention. When he was carried across St. Peter's Square or through the basilica, all the people could see him, including short persons stuck behind broad shoulders. John felt rather unhappy on the shaky throne. "It's windy up here," he sighed over the heads of the crowd. And in private he confessed yet another reason for his dislike for the pompous papal sedan chair: nature had made him fat, and he was always afraid he'd be dropped on the ground.

Roncalli's successors have since done away with the *sedia gestatoria*—along with the white ostrich-plume fans, the guards in their splendid costumes accompanying the pope, as well as the triple crown and the whole coronation ceremony. Paul VI, Giovanni Montini, did let himself be crowned, but shortly afterwards sold off the tiara and gave the proceeds to charity. John Paul I, Albino Luciani, skipped the ritual coronation altogether and staged an "installation" instead. John, who loved old ceremonies, wasn't daring enough to simply give up the golden *sedia*; so he did something that was typical of him—he gave it a new, much simpler meaning. On his coronation day he reminded himself how his father had once carried him on his shoulders, so that he could see a procession in the peasant village of Ponte

Cardinal Masella hands the newly elected pope the
key to the Lateran Basilica, his episcopal church
in Rome on October 28, 1958. *Courtesy* AP

San Pietro. "Once again I am being carried, lifted up by my sons. More than seventy years ago I was carried in Ponte San Pietro on my father's shoulders . . . The mystery of all things is to let oneself be carried by God and thus to carry him to one's brothers."

These are the kind of simple sentences that reveal the mystery of Roncalli. Anyone who believed as simply and powerfully as this Lombard peasant didn't need to barricade himself behind fences or precautionary measures or rigid rituals. He could develop personal initiatives without immediately envisioning the end of the world if he failed to push them through. He trusted his own ideas but he could still delegate power.

Pius XII, conscientious and hypercritical, reserved to himself all even slightly important decisions. He didn't want "collaborators, but executors." He typed his own fair copies of his speeches and had a horror of spontaneous developments that escaped his control. Not that he was a born tyrant, but his respect for the papal office practically crushed him. John was every bit as self-aware as Pius. He was quite clear that the cardinals' choice of him as pope incorporated the will of God; but he understood the Petrine office, quite correctly from the perspective of its New Testament sources, as a kind of dialogue: Peter as someone who strengthens, encourages, and motivates his brothers.

John reintroduced regular conferences with the leaders of the various curial bodies, which had fallen into almost complete disuse with Pius. Scarcely had he been elected than he sketched out the agenda for the first week of his administration. He assured his astounded coworkers that naturally they could call him up any time. He made new appointments for important posts in the Vatican central office that had remained vacant under Pius XII. That included the secretary of state, whose role Pius XII had taken on himself, starting in 1944. A few weeks after his election he named twenty-three new cardinals and in the course of his reign he increased the membership of the College several times, blithely abolishing the limit of seventy wearers of the purple that had been customary for centuries. The British ambassador to the Holy See, Sir Marcus Cheke, noted with surprise that it was, of all people, the spontaneous *causeur* John who made the Vatican efficient again, after it had sunken into chaos under the always correct but autocratic Pius. Word soon got around among Vatican employees that the pope was willing to meet with his staff at any time, but that he mercilessly rejected memoranda and project descriptions more than two pages long.

John XXIII found no harm whatsoever in giving important promotions to people who weren't on his side. He relished contradiction and didn't like to make decisions without hearing different viewpoints. Perhaps it also simply amused him to rub up against his opponents. Perhaps he was in fact so fair or so wise as not to elevate his own opinion to church law and to give other assessments, experiences, and objectives a chance to be heard. At any rate he "never" wanted to speak *ex cathedra* or infallibly. His most surprising coup was to make Domenico Tardini secretary of state on the day after the election. This curial official who was talented but notorious for his brusqueness is said to have resisted, even bringing a medical certificate with him. "I told the Holy Father," Tardini reported, "that I didn't want to serve under him because new methods call for new people, and in the past I had often disagreed with him"—an amiable understatement. Tardini hadn't thought much of Roncalli's diplomatic gifts, and had seldom failed to make this clear. The employees in the Secretariat of State supposedly had a hectic night blotting out all of Tardini's malicious marginal comments on the reports sent by the one-time Parisian nuncio.

The pope listened to all the objections with a friendly nod—and insisted that he wanted Tardini unconditionally: "We're both priests, you and I, and we have to obey God's will." Appointing Tardini was a clever move. Roncalli lacked experience in the curial power game, and in Tardini he was signing onto his team one of its most important men, thereby showing respect and sympathy to the mistrustful curia. The two men are said to have worked together fruitfully and well. Tardini died in 1961, two years before his superior.

In his new Vatican environment Pope Roncalli sometimes seemed like a country pastor out of his element. One day a visitor went astray in the many suites of rooms in the Apostolic Palace and to his utter despair found himself in a hall whose walls were covered with mirrors. At every turn he saw only his own likeness, but no door to escape through. Then with an ungodly creaking noise one of the gigantic wall-mirrors opened up; and the pope himself slipped into the room, raised a finger to his lips and whispered reassuringly, "Psst, I'm lost too!"

Untroubled and unaccompanied, he strolled through Vatican City. He preferred to converse casually with workers and gardeners. There's a wacky story that might actually be true about some furniture packers, who were handling the pope's move from Venice to Rome and dragging chests through the Apostolic Palace when John popped up in one of the rooms and said in his grandfatherly way, "I'm not disturbing you, am I, children?" One worker, who was bent beneath a huge container, thought it was his buddy talking and growled, "Cut the nonsense and just help me!" John obediently started to lend a hand, when the packer looked up, turned red as a beet and stuttered, "Holiness, Holiness!" John cheerfully told him to think nothing of it—after all they both belonged to the party of the strong, squarely built men. Supposedly he then invited the whole group to dinner.

But he also spoke out freely when something didn't suit him. Once plumbers were installing some pipes near the pope's private suite, and one of them let loose an abominable string of oaths. The pope, so the rumor goes, quietly opened the door of his study and politely remarked, "Do you have to do that? Couldn't you just say 'shit' or 'damn it,' the way our kind does?"

Pope Roncalli got rid of the prescribed three genuflections in private audiences ("Do you think I didn't believe you the first time?") and forbade the horrified editor-in-chief of *L'Osservatore Romano* to use the hitherto customary papal titles: "the illuminated Holy Father," "the Chosen one with his sublime lips." The sober-minded Roncalli didn't want to be called *that*. Pius XII's printed speeches had been introduced, in all seriousness, by the recurrent formula, "We reproduce the text of the words of the Holiness of Our Lord, *così come l'abbiamo potuto raccogliere dalle auguste labbra*, as we were able to gather them from his exalted lips."

The fact that he invited guests to lunch offended his stiff chamberlains. But John was unruffled, replying that he couldn't find any passage in Holy Scripture requiring him to take his meals alone. Christ, too, liked to eat with others, he said. Of course, the pope picked up from his table companions many bits of news that his staff would have gladly withheld from him.

Unannounced, he would stick his head into the Vatican carpentry shop, order wine for the workers, and glow when they drank to the health of their new chief. When he invited the newly sworn-in recruits to the Swiss Guard, he is said to have personally phoned a Roman delicatessen and ordered an exquisite feast. But he wasn't content with friendly gestures. John asked his employees about their salaries and families, and found the wages paid by the Vatican were cruelly low. The salaries were raised, so that the ones who earned the least and had the most children got the largest increment. For each child there was an immediate addition of 12,500 lire a month—and scholarships for the gifted younger generation.

Some prelates with doctorates are said to have reacted sourly because a Vatican doorman with loads of kids was suddenly making more than they were; but Pope John was notoriously deaf to this sort of criticism. There were also coworkers who warned him that extra expenses could only be financed by cutbacks on charitable activity. "Then we'll just have to limit the charity," Roncalli dryly countered, "justice come before charity."

He had an especially cordial relationship with the gardeners. He loved to walk around the greenery, but he had no strict schedule as had his predecessor Pius XII. When Pope Pius went strolling in the Vatican gardens, at the same hour every day, the cupola of St. Peter was closed to tourists, to spare the pope their curious glances—amplified, perhaps, through binoculars. John considered such protective measures completely superfluous. "I promise you, I won't do anything improper," he calmed the people in charge. "All clowning and tomfoolery," he sighed at the pretentious telegrams of thanks drawn up by the Apostolic Chancellery in response to congratulations on his election. "Just strike out these extra flourishes. Be simpler, be more cordial!"

"At least try to," he added a little resignedly. "Simplify what's complicated and don't complicate what's simple" was his motto. In his diary he kept admonishing himself, "Angelo, don't take yourself too seriously!"

Giovanni Ventitresimo had little use for the red satin slippers usually worn by his predecessors. One of his first official acts was to have the shoemaker make him a pair of solid street shoes—which were then dyed red to satisfy the venerable tradition. And he was the first pontiff in exactly ninety-nine years to board a train—on the eve of the Council, to make a pilgrimage to Assisi and Loreto—thereby putting an end to the self-imposed imprisonment of the popes in the Vatican.

Roncalli's simple, so-called impromptu talks on street corners when he visited the parishes of Rome, his warm-hearted visits to hospitals and prisons were more effective than speeches on general principles or encyclicals. The world witnessed a deeply personal, accessible Holy See, run by a kindly, pious father figure. "I am Joseph, your brother," he described himself, using an old biblical image. He was *il parocco del mondo*, parish priest to the world—and in that role he made his way into church history.

As late as Lent, 1962, a few months before his death, the eighty-one-year-old pope drove every Sunday to a different working-class parish on the outskirts of Rome. On the way back, he had the habit of stopping here and there and improvising a brief sermon, both pious and witty, for the people assembled on sidewalks and balconies. Former Prime Minister Giulio Andreotti recalls one such off-the-cuff speech on the piazza in front of the church of St. Don Bosco in the Tuscolano quarter. The pope had already preached in the church; but after mass he found the piazza full of people, so he called for a microphone one more time. "He turned first," says Andreotti, "to the children and thanked their parents for bringing them in such numbers to greet the pope. Then he admonished the young people to be good to their neighbors. By that he meant old folks, he explained, because there was no need for exhortations to be good to the girls."

When he wanted to visit someone in Rome, he secretly fetched his chauffeur so that Vatican officials wouldn't ask for a police escort and have the streets closed off. The doorman of an old age home for priests on Monte Mario was astonished when the pope suddenly rang the bell. On his first Christmas in office he appeared unannounced after midnight mass in the Roman children's hospital *Bambino Gesú*, and got an enthusiastic reception from the little patients: "Hello, pope, come here!" they called out. One little squirt wanted to know:

"You, pope, what's your real name?" The Holy Father answered obediently: "When I was a child I was called Angelo; in the army they ordered me around as Giuseppe, and now I'm Giovanni."

He sat for a long time at the bed of a boy who had lost his sight. "We're all blind sometimes, my boy," he said. "Perhaps you'll have the gift of seeing more than others do.

The next day he visited the 1,200 prisoners in the Roman prison Regina Coeli. The Holy Father tipped his zecchetto and greeted them with the words: "You couldn't come to me, so I'm with you." He hadn't brought along any lessons, just memories of his childhood—he used to go around firing away with a slingshot—and of his family. Oh God, once a relative of his had been locked up too for poaching. "How that impression was engraved in me, when the carabinieri came! Now I've come here to the prison," he continued,

> you have seen me, we have looked one another in the eye, and our hearts have come near each other. You may be sure that our meeting will continue to have an effect on me too. Your next letters home will mention how the pope came to see you and at his next mass he will think especially of you, your wives, your sisters, and your families.

Even the cells of murderers and sex offenders, which had been locked for the pope's visit, had to be opened for him: "What does that mean? They're all God's children." One of the criminals, who had a human life on his conscience, looked at him through tear-swollen eyes and stammered that there was probably no more hope for him. Instead of an answer John bent down to the prisoner kneeling before him and gave him a bear hug. After that Christmas the Romans spoke only of *Papa Roncalli*, calling him *Giovanni il buono*, John the Good.

9

A Real Christian
Becomes Pope

*He walked in the presence of God, the way someone
usually walks through streets of his home town.*

—*a journalist from the* Daily Mail

DISCIPLINE, SIMPLICITY, AND critical self-scrutiny shaped his working day in the Apostolic Palace, as it had elsewhere. He got up around four o'clock in the morning, sometimes even earlier. "Prayer goes so well at first light, when everything is quiet," he once said happily. In Venice he had had a terrace built on the roof of his official residence, where at sunrise he liked to pray lauds, the Church's morning prayer, looking down at the sea and the roofs of the old city.

Roncalli was accustomed to spending a lot of time over the newspapers at breakfast—milk, fruit juice, sometimes coffee, rolls, an apple—and taking a brief siesta in his chair. After that, the audiences, which had begun around nine o'clock in the morning, were continued and not infrequently spilled over into long conversations. In the evening he sometimes watched a TV program or took a walk in the garden. He went to bed at around 10 p.m., if there was no pressing work to be done.

He always had to have his mementos and pictures around him, the photographs of Sotto il Monte, the portraits of his parents, the icons from Istanbul, the statue of St. Mark, the patron of Venice, and the diaries, carefully laid out in a little chest of drawers. John was open, spontaneous, ready for surprises, and yet a creature of habit, like many Italians. Every Friday at 3 p.m., the traditional hour of

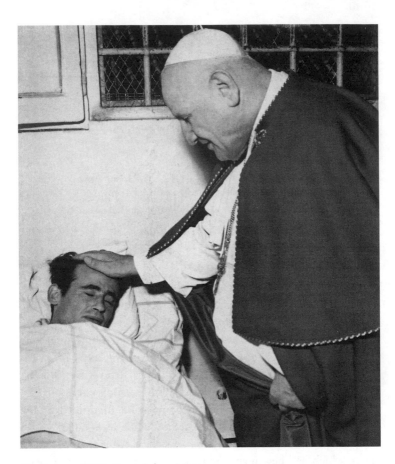

Christmas, 1958, Pope John visits
the central prison in Rome, Regina
Coeli (here the sick bay), and has the
cells of the murderers unlocked.
Courtesy Giordoni

Christ's death on the cross, he made his confession to his spiritual adviser, Monsignor Alfredo Cavagna, a cultured, sober, but deeply pious man, two years older than himself.

In her collection of essays, *Menschen in finsteren Zeiten* (People in Dark Times) Jewish sociologist and political scientist Hannah Arendt dedicates a respectful chapter to Pope John—alongside Karl Jaspers, Rosa Luxemburg, and Bertolt Brecht. She recalls a Roman chambermaid who, when Angelo Giuseppe Roncalli lay on his deathbed, told her in stunned surprise: "Madame, this pope was a real Christian. How is that possible? And how could a real Christian ever get to sit on St. Peter's chair? Didn't he first have to be made a bishop, then an archbishop, then a cardinal, before he finally got elected pope? Didn't anyone have any idea who he was?"

Perhaps they really didn't know much about him—until his *Giornale dell'Anima* appeared, his "Diary of the Soul." But here too the information about the depths of his inner life is kept relatively discreet, and most of the entries date from his days in the seminary and in Istanbul. Young Angelo Roncalli reveals a rather anxious, quite conventional piety, full of scruples and defense mechanisms. In order to safeguard "holy purity," the fifteen-year-old vows to walk through the city with the greatest care, to keep his eyes "lowered, when necessary, to the ground," to ignore store windows with "shameless" contents, to avoid "gatherings of people at celebrations and the like," and looking at any pictures and statues in church, "where the law of decency is disregarded, even to the slightest extent." He wants to be "as pure as an angel." The precautionary measures that he takes remind one of young girls in horror movies trying to fend off nighttime attacks from vampires: "In the evening before going to sleep I will lay the rosary of the Blessed Virgin around my neck, cross my arms on my chest and try to wake up in the same position the next morning." He admires Saint Charles Borromeo who went to confession twice a day and forbade himself any lapses in vigilance because "the devil is smarter than I am."

Still the diary shows how this angst-ridden, terribly rigid form of religiosity was already paired with realistic self-evaluation and the capacity to work on concrete behavioral changes, instead of endlessly pitying himself. Roncalli knows his own weaknesses, he wants to "play the clever one, to judge everything and make my opinion constantly prevail." He liked to talk idly and had to learn to hold his tongue: "I take myself for a seraph, but instead I'm just a little Lucifer full of pride . . . ." And the love for Jesus, the longing for a life close to God, the sense of responsibility of a future priest, bit by bit replaced the initial fear and ego-weakness as his prime motivation.

Angelo was twenty-one years old and back in the Roman seminary from military service when he made a rather radical break with the ideal of holiness he had followed till then. Before making any decisions or after falling into transgressions he had always imagined how St. Aloysius or some other heavenly model would behave—and thus preprogrammed his own failure. "It's a false system," he now acknowledged.

> I have to borrow what's essential in the virtue of the saints and not the incidentals. I'm not St. Aloysius and I don't have to sanctify myself exactly the way he did, but the way that my different nature, my character, and my different conditions of life demand. I don't have to be some meager, thin copy of a type, however perfect. That's how God wants us to follow the example of the saints, by making the vital pith of their virtue our own, to transform it into our blood and to adapt it to our special aptitudes and circumstances.

Shortly after the pope's death Newman scholar Franz Michel Willam went through his unpublished works to find out how his guiding idea of *aggiornamento*, which was so important for the Council, had developed. It was to make the old truths fruitful for a new age, to distinguish between unchangeable substance and time-bound ways of expression. Willam discovered a crucial clue in the just-cited diary entry. For Roncalli this insight meant a giant leap forward in the life of faith, away from imitation and copying one model or another, toward creative imitation. Pious peasants like the Roncallis habitually come before God with a certain self-consciousness: here I stand, your creature but also your partner. Self-tormenting religious masochism is alien to them. This healthy tradition of piety, however, had to assert itself in the face of entirely different traditions, such as those that marked Catholic seminary education around the turn of the twentieth century. *"Dio è tutto: io sono nulla,"* he wrote two years before his ordination in his diary. *"E per oggi basta."* "God is everything, I am nothing, and that's enough for today."

It seems as if the extinguishing of his own personality was his highest goal at the time. But was it so illogical to try to block the overestimation of oneself? The beauty of the world had been there long before his birth. Stars, mountains and seas, animals and people, he noted as an eighteen-year-old in the Bergamo seminary, "beneath the watchful eye of divine Providence, all things on earth proceeded on their orderly path. And I? I didn't exist. Everything fulfilled itself without me; no one thought of me, not even in a dream, because I wasn't there."

What was this little person called Angelo Roncalli worth? The world would go on turning without him. "What else am I but an ant, a grain of sand? So then why do I make myself great in my own eyes? . . . I am nothing and I consider myself a great man. I come from nothing and I'm proud of myself because of the gifts that God has granted me. I am to serve my Creator and instead . . . I serve my ambition, my self-esteem. . . . Lord, hear this blind man, who, as you pass by, calls out loudly to you, begs you to heal him, you who are the light of my eyes!"

The longing overcomes the self-doubt, love drives out fear. Young Angelo increasingly learned to accept himself with his weaknesses and strengths, to calmly work on himself and not let his confidence be taken away:

Stick to a few special prayer exercises, but firmly. . . . Always maintain cheerfulness, serenity and freedom of spirit in everything. When I observe that I am being true to my resolutions, I will praise God from the heart for bringing all this into being. If I should fail, I will absolutely not be disheartened. . . . A fall is followed by an act of deep humility, then I'll begin anew gladly and always with laughter, as if Jesus had caressed me, had encouraged me, and lifted me up again with his own arms.

This was jotted down during the retreat of 1902 after his military service. We already see the Roncalli we know from later on, radiating God's goodness.

"Sins and melancholy, get out of my house," he orders, quoting the comedically gifted Philip Neri, one of his favorite saints. "So let there be no fear, and no castles in the air: not many ideas, but right and serious ones, and still fewer wishes." The striving for equilibrium—"For me that is the toughest nut to crack"—leads to the willingness to deal compassionately with his own inadequate self, but with his fellow men and women as well, "to be forbearing with everyone and condemn no one."

That was by no means always easy for him. Roncalli had a sharp, ready wit, which could sometimes be wounding. Perhaps his strongest antagonist in the Roman curia was Cardinal Alfredo Ottaviani, head of the Holy Office. A rock of pre-conciliar theology (he called himself a watchdog), unbending but humanly engaging, Ottaviani was a baker's son from Trastevere, the quarter where many of Rome's poor lived, and where along with his curial activity he maintained an orphanage. "Alfredo is a very dear friend," said the pope to the ever-present Andreotti. "Too bad he's half blind and has a double chin that sloshes around like the lagoon of Venice when the scirocco blows."

But far more often this sarcasm was aimed at himself. During the Council he had prepared a French speech for a large bishops conference. When its spokesman addressed him in Latin, he wanted to be polite, so he spoke Latin too. The improvised translation from the French didn't go very well. As he was leaving the audience chamber he whispered to the bishops: "*Oggi abbiamo fatto una brutta figura!*"—Today we really looked bad."

As a bishop, as a diplomat, and as pope, Angelo Roncalli remained a self-critical person. He noted at age sixteen that Jesus seemed to him "almost strange," because his thoughts were often somewhere else. Five years later he describes himself as standing before Christ at the Last Judgment, where he unrelentingly lists all the things that will come to light: "proudly going around with a look of erudition, that well-rehearsed, exaggerated restraint, the neatly tucked-in soutane, the shoes in the latest fashion . . . the quiet emergence of envy in fleeting thoughts, the castles in the air . . ."

As a forty-five-year-old in Bulgaria, he sighed that he was simply too inclined to talk. True, that was a gift of God, but he should make use of it only "when people want it from me, and not to satisfy my inclination"—and he had to strive "to leave behind an impression of dignity, kindness and lovableness." Even during the retreat to prepare himself for the end of his eightieth year Pope John says that he is deeply troubled: "so much wretchedness: in putting my energies to work I have in no way matched the vast supply of power that I received. . . . Before the Lord I am a sinner, I am dust." And he was still afraid of sexuality. In this area "God's grace never allowed a temptation and a fall, never, never."

But his erstwhile fear of being damned—in 1902 came the terrified question: "Good Lord, am I to go to hell too?"—had long since given way to an unconquerable trust. He remarks in his Spiritual Testament simply, but definitely, that he is on his way to heaven.

The traits of neurotic self-torment clearly faded with increasing age, giving way to a cheerful serenity. "*Lasciare tempo al tempo*, you have to give time time" was one of his favorite sayings. Why the hectic rush? Why the constant fussing over one's image? In a letter from Paris to his niece Giuseppina Nuncio Roncalli says that it's much better to calmly "let others overtake you with loud shouts" and "waste no time with gossip," but "move forward, always briskly and gaily, as if singing, so that everyone likes us and we are an obstacle to no one."

The following oft-told anecdote may not be literally true, but it makes a point. On the evening when he announced the opening of the Council, Pope John couldn't get to sleep. Finally he called himself to order: "Angelo, why aren't you sleeping? Who's running the Church, you or the Holy Spirit? So sleep!" And he did.

The same is true of the other story about the worries that disturbed him and made him decide to discuss them with the pope. Then he suddenly remembered that *he* was the pope. "Well, good, then I'll talk them over with our Lord," and the burden slipped away from his soul.

John the Good entered the world no more perfect than anyone else. He had to struggle with his own unfulfilled longings, with the humiliations he received from uncomprehending superiors. But he was clever enough to look upon the struggle as a school—and poverty as a bit of freedom. Anyone who is free from all human certainties, free from the compulsion for success, from the pressure to achieve and the need of recognition, poor before God and dependent upon him alone—that person can believe as Pope John did.

In March of 1959 Pope Roncalli moved the participants of a women's congress by telling them that he owed a large part of his vocation to his Bergamask family, "to the example, that our good parents, papa and mama, always gave our heart, and to the whole atmosphere of goodness, simplicity and honesty that we breathed in from early childhood." John still used the plural of majesty, which was kept until his successors Albino Luciani and Karol Wojtyla abandoned it in 1978. But he always remained conscious of his peasant roots—even when it came to his choice of words. The end of life, he brooded after the death of his mother, would be "a stopping in the middle of a furrow."

When asked what he would like to do (at a time when he was already harboring the disease that killed him) once the Council was over, he answered yearningly, "To spend a whole day with my brothers tilling the fields again!" And when Frère Roger Schutz, the prior of Taizé, frankly told him that "people with a Gospel mentality" were repelled by the pomp of the Vatican, he sadly replied, "Our family is a poor family. Do you think I'm not suffering here in the Vatican?" But, he added, he couldn't change everything in a few years.

Poverty and simplicity ran like a red thread through Roncalli's diaries and letters. When he was appointed a papal envoy to Bulgaria, he wrote to his parents from Sofia: "Ever since I left home about ten years ago, I have read many books and learned many things that you couldn't have taught me. But the few things that I did learn from you are the most precious and important: they give all the rest warmth and support . . ."

Meanwhile the simplicity that he embodied and preached was infinitely removed from the *sancta simplicitas* of pious dolts. It had a lot to do with cleverness, with life experience, with wisely limiting oneself to what's permanent. On his sixty-seventh birthday in Paris Roncalli wrote: "To limit everything to the essentials—principles, goals, position, duties—to reach the highest possible simplicity and inner peace . . . and to aim straight for what is truth, justice, and compassion, indeed, compassion above all. Any other way of acting is just posturing and the desire to show off, which soon betrays itself and becomes an obstacle and ridiculous."

There could be no better medicine against the poison of ecclesiastical careerism than this connection to his roots in a poor family of agricultural workers. And when John XXIII talked about poverty, this had little to do with the social romanticism beloved in some pious circles. John directs our view to the "power of the poor," to their "inner riches"—but this power enables them among other things, to fight for the improvement of their wretched living conditions. In the letters to his family Roncalli shows that he knows exactly how much pain the bitter winters bring in the mountain country of Lombardy, what a catastrophe a failed harvest meant, and how humiliating it is to have to till someone else's land.

"Poor, but born the child of honorable and modest people, I am especially glad to die poor," he confesses in his Spiritual Testament, composed while he was still in Venice. This poverty gave him the power, "never to beg for anything, neither jobs nor money nor favors." He had been able to support his family, but only "as a poor man among the poor"—and the fact that he never had to be ashamed of them "is their true title of nobility."

But there is yet another, longer and fuller testament, also written in Venice, and attested to by the seventy-nine-year-old pope. In it he makes very detailed arrangements for the fields and vineyards in Sotto il Monte that still belonged to him and that would now pass on to his brother Giuseppino, and about the little bit of money "that might possibly belong to me upon my death," which he wills to the next pope, to the episcopal curia in Bergamo, to the national central committee of the *Propaganda Fide*, to the kindergarten in Sotto il Monte—and to his sister Maria as well as to his niece Enrica "for whatever needs she might have . . . with the request not to forget the poor, above all the very poor and those among them who feel embarrassed by it."

Had they really known him—the skeptics who thought him clueless and naïve, and the many others who revered him like a reflection of heaven? Wasn't what people took to be an inborn talent, the cheerful optimism of a simple genius, really the fruit of a strenuous effort to see the good and not the bad, to give human beings and the world a chance, because otherwise life makes no sense?

"I trust my eyes," he insists in a letter from Sofia, "I interpret everything in a good sense and prefer to rejoice in the good rather than needlessly let myself be confused by the sight of the evil." It sounds so loose; and yet it presupposes exhausting work on his own ego, which, as we have seen, painfully felt defeats, insults, and injuries.

"If God made the shadow, it was to emphasize the light." Heaps of such commonplace bits of wisdom can be found in John's correspondence. But these banal truths produced astonishing concrete results, for example when it came to the danger of communism. "Yes, we stand facing a Goliath," he confessed to the "hawks" among church leaders. "But he isn't so strong, he isn't superior to us; because he is the embodiment of error, desire, and violence." For this reason the giant would sooner or later have to bow down to God's will. In addition it was false to characterize the Communists as enemies of the Church. The Church had no enemies.

In the spring of 1960 an artist entered the Vatican in order to make a bust of Pope John; it was his compatriot from Bergamo, Giacomo Manzù. There was no more famous sculptor in Europe, but in the pope's entourage people were murmuring once again. Manzù was a Red, from a dirt-poor family, winner of the Lenin Prize, divorced, remarried to an Austrian woman. He had left the Church enraged over the ideals it made with the Fascists. He had been condemned by the Holy Office for sculpting reliefs of Christ as a naked, all-too-human being.

But in the course of the work the pope and the Communist sculptor became friends. Manzù discovered in the highest representative of the Church that he thought he hated, an exemplary human being. So intensively did he come to grips with the pope that he made seven portrait busts—and smashed three of them. Actually he believed in

The hearts of children flew out to him—eight-year-old Catherine Hudson from Oklahoma City, incurably ill with leukemia, in 1962, in her communion dress, on a visit to John XXIII. Her greatest wish was to see the "good pope." *Courtesy* Felici

Federal Chancellor Konrad Adenauer considered John XXIII politically naïve—visit from the German government head on January 30, 1960. *Courtesy* Giordani

nothing, only in humanity, Manzù told a German journalist, who wondered why he was depicting the pope, of all people. Why not? The pope had sought him out. But then, Manzù added very seriously, this man simply loved everybody, even the atheists. "Through him I've learned to be better."

Manzù was allowed to cast the twenty-two-foot-high bronze doors in the vestibule of St. Peter's through which the dead cardinals are borne and which for this reason are called *la porta della morte*, the door of death. He showed death in all its destructive violence, in many forms. He showed the dying Christ and the Madonna at the hour of her passing into the beyond—and within this panorama of death he shows the living Johan XXIII, prostrate in prayer, with a walking staff that is sprouting flowers. Is that an image of the Church on pilgrimage, always renewing itself?

During the work on the giant double door Don Giuseppe De Luca died. He was a humanistically trained writer and a charming person who had set up the contact with the pope. Manzù was profoundly sad, but once again John preached no sermons to him. He said only one thing: "Tears can turn into pearls."

"I see only tears," replied the sculptor.

"The other will come," the pope very gently responded.

"How so, Holiness?"

"You'll see that too. Perhaps on your bronze door."

Wisdom of the heart. Simplicity. Open concern for others. Delicate feeling that avoids poses. After a banquet John reprimanded his secretary Capovilla, a thin ascetic who would and did go through fire for him: "You mustn't put your hand over your glass when they want to pour you wine, that's showing off. Your companions at table will think you're trying to be better than they, which you aren't. Nor am I. Let them pour you some wine, and then in God's name leave it in your glass." Wisdom, simplicity, sensitivity—and, radiating over it all, a compelling kindness.

The one-time German Channel II correspondent Luitpold A. Dorn spoke with Roncalli's house servant Guido Gusso, whom he took with him from Venice to the Vatican. "By that time," Gusso recalled, "when I began to work for him in Venice, I was twenty years old, and naturally I wanted to have a little fun too. I lived in the house with him, and sometimes I came home late. I had a girlfriend, maybe I had been at a film festival or the opera. But I always had to get up at 7 a.m. to serve him at mass, because that was one of my responsibilities too. Sometimes it happened that in the morning he'd knock on my door to wake me up. But then he'd show a lot of understanding and add, 'Ah, you're young and you have to sleep a lot.'"

"Didn't he ever get angry at you?" Dorn asked.

"Never!"

Then Roncalli became pope, and his servant Gusso tried to kneel down before him every time he came up to him, as the custom was. John immediately took him aside and said, "Listen, the two of us will make a deal. When you come to me in the morning, then you kiss my ring. If you want to kneel down, then go to the chapel and kneel down in front of the Blessed Sacrament. In the evening before you leave, kiss my ring again—but I don't want to ever see you kneeling in front of me again."

When he was still the nuncio in Paris, he learned that an old friend in Bergamo wasn't well. Roncalli spontaneously wrote him: "Dear Monsignor, I stand in spirit in your house with my poor little lamp. With cordial and brotherly sharing in your fears." They were both, after all, at the age "when one begins to say vespers," still wishing "to stay on a bit longer," but resigned to the will of God. The evening sun was no longer burning as it had been at noon, but it shed a clear light full of promise.

On his deathbed he called Loris Capovilla, embraced him almost bashfully, and said in his pain to the man who was weeping uncontrollably: "You got along with my weaknesses, and I got along with yours. We will always be friends, I will protect you from heaven. . . . Once all this is over, rest a little and visit your mother."

Attentiveness, tender kindness—and, as the keynote to his life—a compassion that had dramatic effects on the Church's politics. On the law of celibacy the profoundly conservative Roncalli couldn't be shaken. It was a completely different story when it came to dealing with Italian priests who had come to grief on the vow of celibacy and were now out on the street, ostracized by the Church and with no professional prospects—because the Concordat of 1929 excluded them from government service. It was impossible, for example, even to get a job as a teacher. John had too much respect for his curial officials to override their jurisdiction by fiat. But in individual cases he kept trying to make laicization easier and to find loopholes. "With X we are dealing with an unfortunate man who shouldn't have been ordained," he remarked about one of the requests for laicization that had landed on his desk. "His state of soul makes it advisable to free him from his priestly duties and to give him financial support, so that we can help him withdraw without causing a scandal. He deserves grace from God and man."

He hadn't changed in the almost thirty years since that day, July 12, 1934, when he wrote to his brother Giovanni from Bulgaria that he always strove to reach a balanced judgment: "Justice and injustice in these matters can't be completely separated and sliced through the middle. You do your best: you keep silent; if necessary, you pay back evil with good, and make sure that it continues."

It was neither a bishop nor a theologian who most clearly expressed the mystery of this personality, but a journalist from the *Daily Mail* who wrote after John's death: "He walked in the presence of God, the way someone usually walks through the streets of his home town."

What might look like an enviable disposition or a combination of peasant slyness, diplomatic experience and *savoir vivre* looks upon closer inspection like the fruit of a piety that was as naturally emotional as it was deliberately cultivated. Loving God and wishing to live near him; loving human beings because they are God's children and brothers and sisters to each other; being good because an inner voice moves you to; doing one's duty because this world has to get better; remaining serene because this world is neither the last nor the highest thing. In 1946 at a sermon in the cathedral of Bourges Nuncio Roncalli said: "Our earthly life isn't everything. We don't just exist like animals. God has directed our eyes and our heads toward heaven. . . . We are disciples of Christ who has been dwelling among us for two thousand years. His heart is pierced through, his hands are spread out to embrace us all."

It was a simple and actually quite conventional piety, which took guardian angels and heavenly patrons for granted, which treasured traditional prayers and "mortifications" (in Lent the pope took his coffee without sugar, his butler Gusso reported with fascination, and in Advent there was no sausage) and animated by the longing for eternal happiness.

But this piety was powerful, grounded, and centered on the essentials. It did without sentimentality and the appendages that are so important to anxious souls. In 1954 the Church celebrated the 100th anniversary of the dogma of the Immaculate Conception, of Mary as the virgin and mother of God conceived without original sin. This was a bold theological stroke which—when rightly understood and well explained—says a great deal about the acceptance of this world by the incarnate God and about the value of the person. But it was an idea that was bound to become a bone of contention between Catholics and Protestants.

Shortly before the jubilee Marian associations and particularly zealous theologians unleashed hectic attempts to find further titles of honor for the Mother of God and to institute a new feast day *Regalitas Mariae*, Mary Queen of Heaven. They knew they had Pius XII on their side. Among the bishops signatures were collected calling for the introduction of the feast. But the patriarch of Venice wouldn't sign the petition. "When Jesus died," he dryly observed, "he told John: 'Behold, your mother.' That's enough for faith and the liturgy." Everything else might be "edifying and moving" for some pious souls, yet it might also "irritate" many others. But, above all, this sort of innovation might harm "the effectiveness of apostolic activities aimed at restoring the unity of the holy Catholic Church in the world." Half a year later Pius XII nevertheless put the feast on the calendar of the saints.

As far back as 1902, long before the feminist revolts in theology, Angelo Roncalli had stood up for an image of God with motherly features. "He took me away from the country," he wrote, "as a small boy and provided me with everything I needed, with the care of a loving mother." And he had no need of the exaggerations of over-the-top Mariology. One might say, his faith was so stable that he didn't need any extra safeguards.

Did he never doubt? Did his trust in the good Lord never waver?

Perhaps it did. In all the enthusiastic literature about John, so concerned with harmonious images, Roncalli's faithful secretary, Loris Capovilla, does on one occasion strike a jarring note. On November 13, 1953 the patriarch buried his beloved sister Ancilla in the village cemetery of Sotto il Monte. Before the coffin was nailed shut, he had tenderly kissed her on the forehead, as the old women from the peasant houses murmured the rosary,

In the darkness an autumnal storm was sweeping over the hills and a cold rain fell from the sky. As Roncalli and his secretary hurried back to the train station, Capovilla heard the cardinal muttering in a flat tone of voice: "*Guai a noi se fosse tutto un'illusione*"—Woe to us if it all should be an illusion."

10

The Second Vatican Council

We are not here on earth to guard a museum,
but to tend a blooming garden full of life.

—*Pope John XXIII*

On November 20, 1962 Pope John received Japanese Prime Minister Hayato Ikeda. After the audience the politician said to Cardinal Doi of Tokyo: "I lost my father more than twenty years ago. Today I met my father again."

The example of this kindly pastor in the Vatican would serve for a long time to come as the standard for measuring anyone who ascended the chair of St. Peter to strengthen his brothers and sisters in faith and hope.

Sometimes he seemed naïve or rash, as when he was talking with a couple of cardinals and suddenly blurted out, "So why don't we have a Council?"

And when someone objected that a thing like that would be impossible to organize by 1963, as the pope had suggested, John laconically replied:

"Good, then we'll have it in 1962!"

This scene has been described in a number of versions. In one of them it was supposedly Tardini, the secretary of state, who was the first to be taken into Roncalli's confidence three months after the papal election. John XXIII is quoted as saying, "An inspiration suddenly sprang up in us like a flower . . ." According to another version the word "council" first popped up in a conversation with Capovilla,

In order to pray for blessings for
the Council, which was about to
open shortly, Pope John leaves the
Roman station of Trastevere on his
last pilgrimage to Loretto and
Assisi. *Courtesy* OPA

just two days after the election. The only thing we can be sure about is the date of the public announcement of his intention: January 25, 1959, in the Benedictine monastery of *San Paolo fuori le mura*.

Hardly anybody in Rome realized that on that ice-cold, stormy winter day the annual prayer week for the unity of Christians was drawing to a close. At the center of the worldwide Catholic Church only a handful of incorrigible idealists paid any attention to that. The visit to St. Paul outside the Walls was part of the inaugural program of the new pope, which in the first few months had taken him to the most important basilicas of the city. After mass the cardinals present all gathered in the abbot's living room for a cup of hot bouillon. Then the pope, who seemed uncharacteristically tense and nervous, began to speak about the changes that had taken place in Rome since his student days, about the dangers of the modern world, about the "contradiction between the truth and the good," about the capacity the Church had shown to renew itself in such crisis-filled periods, which intensify intellectual clarity and spiritual vitality. And then, after speaking for half an hour, in broadly sweeping images, as usual, he made the announcement:

> Venerable brothers and beloved sons! Trembling a little, no doubt with emotion, yet with humble determination, we speak out to you the name and the plan of a doubly solemn event: a diocesan synod of the city [Rome] and an ecumenical council for the entire Church.

The cardinals responded with a frozen silence—perhaps they were just flabbergasted. In any event John felt deeply disappointed. "Humanly speaking," he later bluntly complained, "we had actually expected that . . . they would press around us to announce their agreement and their good wishes."

Nothing of the sort. Instead of joyful enthusiasm he reaped weary skepticism, indeed contempt. The next day *L'Osservatore Romano* buried the sensational news somewhere on the inside pages. Cardinal Lercaro, who at other times lead the way with his ideas more than any other Italian bishop, voiced his outrage: John, he

said, was far too impulsive. Only his "inexperience" could have mis-
led him into taking such a thoughtless step, which would ruin his
health. Even Roncalli's good friend Montini in Milan shook his
head. "This holy old youngster," he supposedly told a close
acquaintance over the telephone, "doesn't seem to know what a hor-
nets' nest he's getting into."

An ecumenical Council, the twenty-first in the history of
Christendom and the first since 1869/70, a general assembly of the
Catholic Church, with several thousand bishops, superiors of religious orders, and theologians from all corners of the globe; a gigantic forum for discussion against the background of countless
unsolved problems; a thought-factory for convincing and rousing
answers to the religious crisis of modern times and the questions of
survival facing the planet, from world hunger to nuclear war. And
all this was being thought up, thrust forward, and organized by an
old man who, to speak disrespectfully but rationally, could up and
die any day. Wasn't this notion of a Council just a brainstorm—
spontaneous and ingenious perhaps, but also terribly unconsidered
and chaos-inducing—by a sympathetic old dreamer? Hadn't he
already unmasked himself one time before, when he said, "Without
a breath of holy madness the Church cannot grow?"

They were all wrong. Even Pope John himself was wrong when he
presented the plan for the Council as a momentary impulse, as an
inspiration of the Holy Spirit, as a sudden flash of lightning. *A un trat-
to*, from one moment to the next, his soul had been illuminated by a
"wonderful" thought. Or so he told pilgrims from Venice in May 1962
as he described that mysterious conversation with the now-deceased
Tardini. "And then a word sprang to our lips that was solemn and
binding. Our voice pronounced it for the first time: a Council!"

In his diary several months later, shortly before the beginning of
the Council, he tells the same story: in January, 1959, while conversing with Tardini, he had brought up the idea of calling a council and a diocesan synod (and bringing out a revised edition of canon
law), "without ever having thought of it before and contrary to all
my ideas and imaginings on the subject. The first one to be sur-

prised by my suggestion was myself . . ."

Perhaps. In any case John forgot to add that shortly before his election as pope he had already spoken (as his secretary Capovilla attests) about the "necessity of calling a council," and that a few days later he discussed the same topic with Cardinal Ruffini of Palermo, a spokesman for the conservatives. Maybe these trial balloons actually slipped his mind. He preferred to be surprised by the Holy Spirit and to be forced to adopt the daring plan. Perhaps in his modesty he hadn't clearly realized that the "inspiration"—if it was one—was rooted in the story of his life and in his thought, which was strongly oriented to history.

There was an ancient tradition of collegial government of the Church. It had been buried in oblivion in the West; but it was powerfully alive in the East; and no twentieth-century pope, no cardinal back then, knew this better than the one-time Balkan diplomat Roncalli. Besides, as the bishop's secretary in Bergamo and as a cardinal in Venice, he had already witnessed the spiritual energy that synodal gatherings could unleash. In France he observed the fruitful cooperation among local bishops, who on this score were far ahead of other areas of the world Church. But for Roncalli—experts in Bologna such as Giuseppe Alberigo and Alberto Melloni are convinced—the most lasting impression came from his dealing with Carlo Borromeo and his efforts at translating the impulses and reforms of the Council of Trent into reality in the Bergamo region.

If anyone who could realize this plan, which his predecessors had always somewhat vaguely dreamed about, it was Roncalli. The First Vatican Council had never officially ended; it was merely adjourned in October 1870 because the Franco-Prussian war was threatening to break out, and Piedmontese troops had occupied the Eternal City. One of its major topics had been the relationship between papal and episcopal authority. The Council had awarded the pope an unprecedented abundance of power and, among other things, defined his infallibility (within a clearly limited framework). Lest all this lead to a stifling Roman centralization, many Council fathers wanted to balance out the papal power of leadership with an upward revaluation of episcopal responsibility. But that never happened, not least of all because the critical minority had already left Rome.

On the one hand, therefore, there was a gaping hole in the structure of the Church that finally had to be filled. On the other hand, the supreme papal power proclaimed in 1870 seemed to make any further church assemblies superfluous. The popes saw—and exploited—this dilemma: Vatican I had been able to carry out only part of its agenda, Pius XI reflected in his first encyclical; but "We cannot decide" to take up where it left off until a clear sign from heaven appeared. Naturally, any gathering of the worldwide Church in Rome while Mussolini was in charge would have run into problems.

The next pope, Pius XII, likewise flirted for a while with the idea of a Council. In 1948 two hard-liners whom we have already met, Ruffini in Palermo and Ottaviani in the Vatican, drew up a memorandum with a rather defensive program: the Council would reject the numerous errors prevalent in philosophy, theology, morality, and social teaching. It would take a position on communism, it would reform canon law, and perhaps declare Mary's Assumption into heaven a dogma (which Pius XII did on his own in 1950). Ottaviani's Holy Office established a few secret commissions that put together a variegated palette of subjects—from existentialism to Darwin, from sacred virginity through the dangers of masturbation to psychoanalysis and labor unions. But when yet another representative team of bishops from around the world was consulted, and they tried to put an immense number of new problems on the agenda, Pius XII had enough. He cut off the discussion, condemned the "errors" cited by the preparatory commissions in his encyclical *Humani generis*—which caused so many headaches for the French bishops and Nuncio Roncalli in Paris—and henceforth reserved to himself the right to give the Church its marching orders.

John XXIII had completely different ideas about a council—and for that reason he also managed to make it happen; because in his view a council was supposed to do what no pope or curial commission was capable of. He had learned from church history that this sort of gathering of Christians had something to do with memory, self-cleansing, and getting back to one's roots, rather than just piling up condemnations of contemporary ideas. "We are not on the earth to guard a museum," he had once said about the Church, "but to tend a blooming garden full of life."

John considered it relatively unimportant to confirm the descent of humanity from a single primordial couple or to discuss the precise value of baptism when administered by a non-Catholic, as the Holy Office had proposed doing. He was driven by the question of how the Church could respond better to its vocation. "For two thousand years Christ has been hanging with outspread arms on the cross," he said to Capovilla on the evening before making the public announcement about the council in St. Paul. "How far have we gone in proclaiming the Good News? How can we bring his authentic teaching home to our contemporaries?"

In a message to the clergy of Venice in April, 1959 John compared the Council to the apostles gathered together in Jerusalem after Christ's resurrection and ascension: the point was to "toughen and renew [the powers of the Church] in the search for what best meets the requirements of the apostolate today." Two months later the pope informed the students of the Greek College in Rome that with the Council the Church was seeking "to win new strength for its divine mission," the Church that "even in the face of today's demands consolidates its life and its cohesion with zealous enthusiasm."

Doggedly, stubbornly, Roncalli pushed his plan for the Council without much support from his coworkers, filling out the idea with his own goals: self-discovery and renewal of the Church in a changed world, dialogue with the challenges of the times, and rapprochement with the separated confessions. John, that icon of humility who was capable of both critically scrutinizing his own person as well as of delegating power, had a thoroughly healthy self-consciousness. The task of the conclave was clear: it was God's will that he should lead and decide. "I am not afraid of opposition, and I am ready to suffer," he told his secretary as they spoke about resistance to the council. "I have a program in my mind, and I'm now longer talking around this issue. I am in fact firmly decided."

The opposition went beyond the walls of the Vatican; and it

would be too simple to draw a dividing line between sympathetic, open-minded pastoral bishops like Roncalli and dried up, mistrustful mossbacks in the curial offices. Even among the receptive spirits there were many, as we have seen from the examples of Lercaro and Montini, who thought the plan for the Council was superfluous or half-baked. And the perspective of the curia was then, as it is today, often considerably broader and more tolerant than the narrow viewpoint of some bishops conferences.

Nevertheless, the natural need of the authorities was to have peace and quiet, to keep the well-worn machinery running smoothly. Alternative ideas from "outside" or the unconventional notions of an interloper, like Roncalli, who had been elected pope without experience in the curia, were naturally felt to be more a threat than an enrichment. But when the bureaucrats vexed him too much with their objections and attempts to appease him, John dug himself in behind his peasant stubbornness and added, "*Il concilio si deve fare malgrado la curia*—The Council has to get done despite the curia!"

But because he was not just stubborn but sly, he took the wind out of the sails of the faction that opposed him by integrating them into the project. He made the skeptical Tardini president of the preparatory commission while appointing the heads of the Roman congregations as leaders of the working groups who were supposed to break down the enormous range of topics into clearly delineated portions and then deliver the drafts of texts (the so-called *schemata*) for deliberation by the Council.

This inevitably led to what was, for the most part, a horribly boring rehash of traditional scholastic theology, a thick pile of soulless documents with no sense of the actual religious needs of modern people. The central text of the Council was supposed to be a "dogmatic constitution," whose four chapters bore the headings, "On the Sources of Revelation," "On Preserving the Treasure of Faith," "On the Christian Moral Order," and "On Chastity, Marriage, Family, and Virginity." Ottaviani proposed having the Council make a solemn profession of faith, to drive home once again the lesson of the "anti-modernist oath" invented by Pius X, and to condemn all those who spoke with "exaggerated emphasis" about the historical sins of the Church.

On May 11, 1962, John XXII receives from President of Italy
Antonio Segni the peace of the Balzan Foundation. Actually,
the pope observed, the prize was not meant for him,
Courtesy Giovanni

But the Vatican preparatory groups were by no means working in as much of a vacuum as it looked. Letters had been written to the bishops, religious superiors, and Catholic universities all over the world, and exactly 2,150 position papers, textual proposals, and lists of questions had been received and collected in fifteen hefty volumes. Among the more than 800 coworkers on the preparatory commissions there were a few independent thinkers who shared Roncalli's goal of a "new Pentecost." And then Pope John established, almost casually, a *Secretariat to Promote the Unity of Christians*, a completely new kind of curial authority to look into what other denominations thought about the Catholic Church and expected from the Council. That struck some people as unheard of. The German Jesuit Augustin Bea, a half-year older than the pope, but intellectually vibrant and full of creative cunning in dealing with the Vatican bureaucracy, took over the leadership of the secretariat. For coworkers he got experienced ecumenical specialists from all over the world.

The statements sent to Rome by bishops' conferences and theological faculties admittedly leave the impression that many of the people who had been called upon were still unaware of their new possibilities, and they were very hesitant about voicing their expectations. In the commissions most of the proposals that seemed too dynamic were immediately de-fanged.

John let all the "virtuous" drafts stand as they were, and praised the industrious editors. Only once did he sigh, pick up a ruler and say to a confidant, "Look, just twelve inches of condemnations!" Conservative as he was, dealing gingerly with new developments, he never reckoned on a great revolution. Besides, it was part of his humility to give room to people who disagreed with him, and to brake his own eagerness for reform.

And finally, this can't be said often enough: He trusted the Holy Spirit. If it was God's will, then the bishops gathered in Rome would just take hold of the freedom that was theirs. "Who is actually organizing the Council?" the Belgian Cardinal Suenens, a "liberal" mentor, asked the pope, in some concern.

"*Nessuno*," answered John. "Nobody."

But the conciliar planners in the Vatican didn't know that yet.

They had loaded down the bishops coming to Rome with seventy draft texts on every possible issue. It seemed mysterious, but this mountain of material was supposed to be mastered in a few weeks. The curia had already issued its warning: the bishops should by no means leave their bishoprics without oversight for too long, and the cost of living in Rome was much too high for envoys from poor dioceses. None of this would pose any problems, if people would just speedily dispatch the prepared texts and dispense with unnecessary discussions.

Things would turn out quite differently.

Stage directors have always envied the Catholic Church for its ability to put on a show. On October 11, 1962 2,540 Council fathers marched across St. Peter's Square to the opening of the Council. It took an hour and a half, a procession that refused to end, a forest of white miters atop faces of every color, and scattered among them the gleaming gold crowns of the Oriental patriarchs. For the first time in history the Church Universal was actually gathering in Rome, with Africans, Asians, and Latin Americans from the young churches of the Third World, not just the missionary bishops from old Europe. Along with them the problems of today's world entered the council hall, the fears and longings of modern men and women, the difficulties that they had with "the old lady Church," and the faint hope for a word that could change the world.

And amid the bishops and abbots from all five continents there was the old pope, who instead of his tiara was wearing a miter like the rest. After the entrance into St. Peter's he got down from his *sedia ges-tatoria*, to proceed to the altar on foot. He wanted to be one of them, a brother bishop, not a pope-king at the head of a ruling clan. He wanted to give them an example, so that the Church could be transformed: a community of the people of God instead of a pyramid of power; God's people on pilgrimage, on the way through history, learning and developing, holy and sinful, still far from the goal, knowing the danger of confusing itself with the Kingdom of God; service instead of power; the obligation to bear witness and not to rule.

St. Peter's was transformed into a sort of parliament, with a rising row of grandstands 300 feet long, headsets, microphones, a public address system, translation equipment, and vote tabulation machines. Near the main altar sat the observers from the non-Catholic churches—this kind of invitation had never been sent before—and the envoys from eighty-six governments and international organizations. In the back rows and up in the galleries clustered the theological advisers brought along by the bishops and the journalists (who were later excluded from the working sessions and had to make do with meager communiqués).

But the rainbow-colored inaugural procession, the 200,000 people out on St. Peter's Square and the millions watching on TV, were only a beautiful—though doubtless eloquent—picture. What remains from this day and what changed the course of church history is the address by the pope. It had been thoroughly prepared and was delivered in Latin in a sonorous voice. It contained the sum of the life experiences of an old man—and at the same time the prophetic vision of a young rebel.

"*Gaudet Mater Ecclesia*"—so begins this speech (which lasted exactly thirty-seven minutes), and that is how it is cited today in all studies of the Council, as though it were an encyclical. "Today Mother Church rejoices," a Church whose vitality had been continually attested to by the previous councils and regional synods. "They strengthened spiritual energies, by leading them upward to the goods that are true and eternal." John trusted that thanks to this Council as well, the Church would "grow in spiritual wealth and, fortified with new energy, look fearlessly into the future."

As the pope went on speaking, the expression on the face of Cardinal Ottaviani, who was sitting alongside him, a man who had grown gray in the office of guardian of the faith, turned to stone. Still more faces nearby were also turning to stone, but on the grandstands of the bishops from 133 countries and on the press benches, ears pricked up: "In the daily exercise of our pastoral office," the pontiff declared solemnly and candidly,

> it often happens that voices make their way to us and offend our ears: voices that are burning, it is true, with religious zeal, but not equally gifted with tact and good judgment. In the current con-

ditions of human society they can see nothing but betrayal and destruction. They say that in comparison with the past our age has done nothing but decline and deteriorate. And they behave as if they had learned nothing from history, which is the teacher of life, and as if in the times of the earlier councils the Christian idea and Christian life, morals, and the just freedom of the Church had done nothing but blossom and triumph.

"But we have to decisively contradict these prophets of doom," John declared amidst the breathless silence, "who keep on predicting nothing but disaster, as if the world was about to end. In the present-day development, in which human society is evidently being led to a new order of things, we should rather see a hidden plan of divine providence, which through the efforts of human beings, but above and beyond their expectations, is pursuing its own goal."

The example that the pope cites here is in itself a provocation: the political and scholarly debates of the present leave very little time for dealing with spiritual, religious things, which is certainly a failing and worthy of censure. On the other hand, under the conditions of modern life many of the obstacles had been swept away that in earlier times had limited the Church's freedom of action. This could be seen, for example, in the undue interference of government authorities in the course of ecumenical councils.

So what was to be done? The main task of this Council consisted in "preserving and presenting the sacred body of traditional Christian teaching *efficaciore ratione*, in a more effective way." The Church must not turn away from the inalienable transmission of the truth, as received by the Fathers. But at the same time it had to take seriously the new conditions and forms of life in the present, which had "opened new paths for the Catholic apostolate."

"Our responsibility," John continued, "is not just to guard this precious treasure, as if we were merely busied with the past. We want to dedicate ourselves zealously and fearlessly to the task posed by our age. In that way we continue on the path that the Church has taken over the course of twenty centuries."

Nor was it the task of the Council to discuss one or another foundational article of faith or to repeat the opinions of the fathers of the church and the theologians. They knew all that, and there was no need of a council to do it. Rather, Christians today were waiting for a richer and deeper understanding of the faith from a "renewed, peaceful, and serene" assent to the comprehensive doctrinal tradition. The Church's teachings—which were sure and immutable—had to be studied and explained in the way that modern times demanded. "For the substance of the tradition of faith is one thing; its formulation is something else."

Of course, there were false teachings and dangerous opinions, and the Church had always condemned them, the pope added, calming the anxious souls in his own ranks. "But today the Bride of Christ [the Church] prefers to apply the medicine of mercy rather than to use the weapons of severity. She thinks that it is more in keeping with the demands of today to present the convincing power of her teaching than to pronounce a condemnation."

On the evening of this historic day 500,000 men and women—Romans, pilgrims, tourists from all over the world—prepared an enthusiastic homage to the "good pope." The Catholic youth of the Eternal City organized a torchlight procession. Twilight had just come on, the moon sailed out from behind a cloud, and that gave John, who was looking down at the crowd from the window of his study on the fourth floor of the Apostolic Palace, the cue for the finest impromptu speech of his life. Even the moon, he joked, had been in a hurry to see the procession. Everyone laughed and applauded.

Happy and moved, with a strong voice the pope went on, "*Cari figlioli, cari figlioli, sento le vostre voci*—Dear children, dear children, I hear your voices! My voice is only one, but it sums up the voices of the entire world."

He spoke of the hopes of the nations—the next day he would call the attention of the assembled delegations from the various countries to the universal "cry for peace"—and of his own expectations of the council. "My person counts for nothing," he protested, when the cries of jubilation became too much for him. "I speak to you as a brother, who through God's will has become a father."

At the end of this address gray-haired workers from the poor suburbs of Rome and young families were not ashamed to weep when he said to them, "So, and now I give you my blessing and allow myself to wish you a good night. And when you get home, give your little children a kiss and tell them it's from the pope. Perhaps you will find you have been crying; then dry your tears and say a good word; the pope is with you!"

The surprises didn't end that day. When the inaugural speech appeared in the *Acta Apostolicae Sedis*, where papal documents are collected and printed in their supremely official form, attentive readers were astonished to see that the text had been altered and smoothed out. For example, the sentence quoted above about the eternal substance and the historically conditioned expression of the deposit of faith now ran as follows: "For the deposit of faith that has been handed down, or the truths contained in the teaching that must be preserved, is one thing; and the way in which they are proclaimed—in the same sense, to be sure, and with the same meaning—is another." This addition was borrowed almost verbatim from the anti-modernist oath of Pius X. In other passages as well Roncalli's splendid challenges were remolded into balanced doctrinal formulas and thus robbed of their point.

Pope John spotted that too, of course; and afterwards he deliberately and repeatedly quoted his speech in the uncensored original version. Meanwhile the Latin address given in St. Peter's was itself a reworking: together with Monsignor dell'Acqua, the papal "court theologian," Father Luigi Ciappi, and an expert on Latin, John had reframed his earlier Italian sketches for the inaugural address in solemn ecclesiastical Latin.

Anyone who compares the speech delivered in St. Peter's, the Latin version that was published later, and the Italian version that was distributed to the journalists and printed in *L'Osservatore Romano* will note, among other things, that the word *balzo* is missing. *Un balzo*, or a "leap forward"—was what John said the Church had to take at the Council, in order to reach a more profound understanding of the faith, to meet the demands of the contemporary world.

Alberto Melloni of the *Istituto per le Scienze Religiose* in Bologna

has evaluated the pope's handwritten and typed notes and recon-
structed an "original version" in Italian of the inaugural address.
The results are unequivocal: the Italian version published in 1962
reflects Roncalli's intentions far more faithfully than the Latin
speech given in St. Peter's, not to mention the official Latin version.
Now we can also understand why John—as Capovilla reports—said,
"I want the first Italian sketch of my speech to be published, not
because I'd like to be praised for it, but because I want to take
responsibility for it. People should know that the speech is mine,
from the first word to the last."

All this was because no sooner had the progressive pope's cunning opponents recovered from their first shock than they began to
spread the rumor that good old John had let himself be duped into
reading out a text with dangerous passages from Cardinal Suenens
or Father Bea.

They knew exactly why they were crusading against an innocent
speech, as if it were the Bible of some new heresy. The thesis of the
speech—a nuanced-to-positive interpretation of contemporary
reality, stressing service to the world as the task of the Church and
pastoral assistance instead of overbearing condemnation—was in
fact paving the way for a new era. With his invitation to read the
signs of the times not just defensively and to see God at work in
contemporary developments, John, as journalist Ludwig Kaufmann
says, "was restoring once more the right and responsibility of
prophecy in the Church."

Speaking to a coworker from his days in Paris, the pope had
confided his hopes of concluding the Council in three months, since
everything had been prepared so well in advance. That idea was
doomed, because the "fathers"—as the Church's representatives
somewhat nostalgically called themselves—were completely hand-
cuffed by the seventy interminable, minutely detailed, theologically
antiquated, and at times terribly out of touch "schemata" of the
preparatory commissions. But to start off by throwing out the texts,
lock, stock, and barrel, would have seemed a rude affront to the
arduous work of the curia and to the pope himself, who had read all
of them and evidently found them in order.

December 2, 1962 John XXIII reads his last Christmas message, another urgent call to the whole world for unity and peace. Although he would celebrate mass three times on the feast of Christmas, the signs of his serious illness are unmistakable. *Courtesy* Felici

And so people began to discuss, to make changes, to prune here and add there. After just a few weeks it was clear that not one of the prepared "schemata" could pass in its original form. A prime example of this was the passionately anticommunist declaration, entitled *De cura pro Christianis communismo infectis* ("On the pastoral care of Christians suffering under communism") and hidden away in the schema "Pastoral Care for Special Groups." Cardinal Alfred Bengsch of East Berlin implored his confrères not to use language like "fear of the Soviets" or "hatred of communism." Such well-meaning solidarity with the persecuted would only worsen their situation.

Then was the embattled tone of the schema *De Ecclesiae Militantis Natura* ("On the Nature of the Church Militant"), which exalted the authority of the hierarchy and treated salvation apart from Rome as unthinkable. In the council hall a Dutch bishop rebuked the authors of this pugnacious text for defending a long outdated triumphalism and for talking like jurists rather than pastors.

Slowly the Council broke free. Groups were formed to consider how to tighten up the program and present their views in selective interventions. Among the mentors of such pressure groups were the Brazilian bishop Helder Câmara, who never took the floor once in the council hall, but who exercised enormous influence behind the scene in favor of a "Church of the poor," Belgian cardinal Leon Suenens, and the archbishop of Milan, Giovanni Battista Montini, who predicted in the magazine *L'Italia* that after the first trial run the next session of the Council would move forward much more quickly. The documents would be condensed, and discussion would be limited to questions "justified by today's pastoral needs" and that "are of general interest."

From day to day the bishops of the Church Universal gained more self-awareness. The Council hall gave them a unique opportunity to get to know one another and to ascertain two things: that the problems and concerns of Christians were more or less the same everywhere; and that headquarters in Rome was not so omniscient and not so well supplied with prescriptions for the future as had been thought.

At the very first working session on October 14 there was an uprising. When the elections for the various conciliar commissions were scheduled to take place, the "fathers" (led by the French bishops and Cardinals Frings of Cologne, Dörpner of Munich and König of Vienna) simply refused to confirm the rosters of the preparatory bodies as presented by the curia. First, everyone had to get acquainted. So the elections were postponed; national bishops conferences formed, common lists were drawn up.

Pope John must have enjoyed the stormy awakening of the drive toward freedom among his episcopal colleagues. He deliberately stayed away from the sessions—his mere presence would likely have hindered some people from speaking openly. But he carefully followed the debates in his study on a closed-circuit TV monitor. The bishops were to freely exchange their opinions and experiences, in keeping with his motto: "We aren't monks singing in the choir!"

The pope intervened only once, but all the more decisively when he did. The debate over the "two sources of revelation"—i.e., about the relative value of Holy Scripture and tradition for the Church—had gotten hopelessly deadlocked. A clear majority of the Council fathers rejected the prepared schema, but they couldn't muster the necessary two-thirds majority to send it back to the commission. In order to break up the ice jam, the pope removed the schema from the order of business and appointed a mixed commission to work out a new draft. As co-chairs of the commission he assigned the old antagonists Ottaviani and Bea—a somewhat rash move, but, as it turned out, a successful one.

Although the pope was excruciatingly respectful of his fellow bishops' freedom of speech, there could scarcely be any doubt about what he was looking forward to. The story of the open window has been told a thousand times: when asked what he hoped from the Council, John flung a window wide open and said, "That it lets in fresh air!" Capovilla has long since unmasked the anecdote as a canard—the pope couldn't bear drafts. But, as the Italians say, *se non è vero, è ben trovato* (if it's not true, it's apposite); and Capovilla agreed.

The pope dreamed of a serving Church, prophetic, unobtrusively bearing witness to its message. He saw the Church not as an end in itself, self-righteous and self-sufficient, but obliged to those who were still searching or who didn't even know what they should be looking for.

He had firmly told the central preparatory commission that the Council was not to be a congress for theological speculation, "but a living, pulsating organism that embraces everyone in the light and in the love of Christ." The emphasis had to be on "what connects us," as he encouraged the Catholic peace movement *Pax Christi* in 1961, "and on walking the road together with everyone as far as possible, without betraying justice or the truth." And at Christmastime in 1962 he told the assembled cardinals about his longing for a Church that would work with fresh enthusiasm for a "new and powerful radiation of the Gospel all over the world."

Finally a note from a conversation on January 23, 1963 could not be clearer: "The Church's representatives do not want to flee to an island or lock themselves up in a fortress; nor do they wish to behave like someone who sees other people and shouts: 'They don't matter to us, let them shift for themselves!' . . . Those who would limit themselves to contemplating the shining heavens and to guarding the truth handed down by their ancestors as a hidden treasure would be going astray. For by doing so they would forget that Christ's arms are lifted up over everyone and everything. Christ has come down to us to sacrifice himself for the salvation of the whole human family."

Aggiornamento was his oft-misunderstood magic word, which is inadequately translated by "change" or "adaptation," and is more clearly understood as "bringing-up-to-date." In Roncalli's view the Church should neither frantically chase after the world nor applaud it uncritically. But an encounter should be possible, free from fear and prejudice. Christians should get out of their defensive posture, their bunker mentality. John in no way defined "progress" as the new dogma; he simply saw God at work in all the vicissitudes of history; and he invited people to join him in perceiving the good "signs of the times. "It's not that the Gospel is changing," he would make clear in his testament. "No, it is we who are just beginning to understand it better."

He wanted a "powerful, shining and fascinating" proclamation of the old truths; and although some considered him a terribly naive optimist, he was aware that, "We live in times and situations where priests and lay people may know the Our Father and the Creed by heart; but they don't understand it, and they don't grasp its spirit."

Most of the Council fathers hardly ever saw the pope, and so they were taken completely by surprise at the end of 1962 when, for the first time, he cancelled all his audiences on the advice of his medical team. This after a severe intestinal hemorrhage, which *L'Osservator Romano* downplayed as "stomach troubles." The doctors told the truth neither to the eighty-one-year-old pope nor to the public. But John, who increasingly suffered pain and was undergoing cobalt radiation treatment, knew very well that it was the disease that had already carried off his mother and brother and four sisters: cancer.

When John XXIII died on June 3 in the following year, the first session of the Council had just ended—there would be four in all. But the assembly of bishops had entered on the precise path that "John the good" had led them to. Walls were, in fact, being torn down, doors were being opened, guidelines being laid out, from which even in the years afterwards there could be no deviating, despite difficulties and powerful counter-currents.

The recognition of other Christian communities as churches, the profession of freedom of religion, the new high regard shown to other religions, the stress on the co-responsibility of the bishops in leading the Church, the recognition of independent lay activities, the solidarity with the longings and sufferings of the age—all this is taken for granted nowadays. It sounds almost banal, but back then it had to be pushed through in Rome amid hard-fought struggles.

The Church of Vatican II doesn't want to live in the ghetto anymore, but to commit itself in and to the world. It no longer wants to be an Isle of the Blest, but the leaven of the earth, the ferment of human development. Henceforth Catholics would, as a matter of course, work together with all men and women of good will for the sake of values that they believe in. The Church talks about God by discovering him in human beings. The Church finds its vocation by going out to people.

Needless to say, the new spirit didn't come over Catholic

Christendom at a stroke. Needless to say, different currents flowed alongside one another; and the results of the Council were mixed, as they always are whenever people head out toward new shores. The Church presents itself as a living community, driven by the power of God, as an organism animated by love and trust—and yet it keeps on clinging to legalistic norms and hierarchical decision-making structures. The discovery of strange treasures takes the place of the old-time fanatical desire to convert everyone. Catholics go out to others, ready to learn instead of waiting for them to knock on church doors—and then they panic again at their own courage, they take refuge in segregation, and throw up barriers, not least of all because good will is no protection against disappointments; and some contemporaries are simply too egotistical, too insensitive, too lazy, too much in love with profit and the good life to take on themselves the demands of faith—however obligingly and invitingly the Church may present itself.

But the Church has found a new relationship to the secular world and this cannot be taken back. The test case is religious freedom. Not long ago Catholics used to say that error had no rights and had to be suppressed for the salvation of immortal souls. Freedom of religion was demanded only for one's own denomination. At the Council, by contrast, the Church solemnly agreed that it was a part of human dignity for every person to be able to believe and act in accordance with his or her conscience.

Karl Rahner called the Council, which as an adviser to the German bishops he helped shape, a "fundamental caesura in the history of Christianity." Something new happened there, "that is universal, that remains." But Rahner also knew that, "Whether in the dull bourgeois complacency of our churchly business we grasp and live this new thing here and now—that's another question. That is our responsibility."

From the outset, understanding among the confessions was one of the goals of the bishops' assembly. When the task of revival was complete, Pope John promised in a speech before diocesan leaders of Catholic Action in Italy, "then we shall present the Church in all her glory, without blemish or wrinkle, and we shall say to all the others who are separated from us, the Orthodox, Protestants, and so forth: Look, brothers, that is the Church of Christ! We have striven to be true to her; and we have prayed to the Lord for the grace that she may always remain as he wanted her to be. Come, take your place or take it back—for a great number of you it was your fathers' place!"

So it was a return to the house of a common father, to a purified and redecorated house, but all the same the Roman Catholic father's house. John XXIII couldn't imagine the end result of ecumenical rapprochement any other way. Today's models of "conciliar unity" or "reconciled variety" were alien to him. Despite that, he took the ecumenical movement, which under his predecessor had been viewed from a suspicious distance, and made it "presentable" to the Vatican.

One must also make allowances for him, in that the ever-vigilant Roman censorship, as we have seen, never spared the pope and, if he wasn't careful, turned his thoughtful initiatives into tame lines from the catechism. In 1959 at San Paolo, *fuori le mura*, when he surprised those around him by proclaiming the Council, he also explicitly issued an invitation "to the believers from the separated churches" "to "join with us in this festive banquet of grace and brotherliness." But lo and behold, the official version published later merely voiced a wish that the "separated communities" (what an outrage that John should recognize them as churches!) might "follow us too, with good will, in this search for unity and grace." No more sharing in a common banquet, just the patronizing recognition of a search for something that they obviously had lost—those black sheep from the barn they had once shared with the rest of us.

John himself had to go through an immense learning process so that he could open his heart in this way. In his diary the twenty-two-year-old seminarian tells how the superior of the house asked him to take some walks with a young Protestant who was preparing to convert to Catholicism. "I feel bad about the poor lad," Angelo writes in dismay: in the "best years" of his young life he had been saturated by the seductive teaching of the "heretics," and now he was full of prejudices. Indeed, "It is enough to spend a few hours with a Protestant" to recognize the value of the true creed and the "danger that threatens our faith in Italy from the insidiousness of the sects."

In 1907 Roncalli was twenty-six years old; in his otherwise quite broad-minded talk on the Baronius tricentennial he reproaches Catholic scholars for dealing "too superficially" with Protestantism and simply illustrating the "material damages" that resulted from the "German revolt." One had to give a more forceful accounting to oneself of "just how far the Lutheran idea had had dissolvent and destructive effects in the very minds [of Protestants], that idea which the monk from Wittenberg had first crudely formulated and which then quickly overpowered even exquisite thinkers and disguised itself in the garments of scholarship . . ."

Even in his first encyclical *Ad Petri Cathedram* in June of 1959 Pope John was still extremely reserved in speaking about "those separated from us, even though they call themselves Christians," and their longing "to reach some form of unity." By its tone, which was (quite atypically for John) defensive, complaining, and authoritarian, this encyclical evidently served as a sop to his Vatican opponents, who as they witnessed his ideas and activities were increasingly given to clasping their heads in horror. A few paragraphs later we find a warm-hearted invitation to the "brothers and sons" to return, and "not to a stranger's house, but to their, common father's house."

John no doubt did his fastest and most important learning as pope. He knew the Orthodox extremely well from his time in Sofia and Istanbul. He was also slightly familiar with the Jews; but now along came the Protestants, then the Anglicans, the underground churches of Communist world, and the other religions, which were competing with Christianity in Africa and Asia.

His familiar brotherly tone toward the observers at the Council from the other Christian churches set a standard. In an eloquent gesture at an audience on the day after the Council opened Roncalli didn't head toward his throne, but took his place in the middle of the room. He told the group about his experiences with Christians of different confessions in the Balkans: "We didn't get into long negotiations, we spoke with one another. We didn't discuss things, but we were well-intentioned toward one another."

John was the first pope for centuries to welcome to Rome Orthodox leaders, representatives of Protestantism, Anglican archbishop of Canterbury, Geoffrey Fisher—and the abbot of the Japanese Buddhist Union. His chief aim in all this was always the search for common ground, as it had been on his diplomatic missions. He didn't want to linger over old disputes about who was to blame.

"We don't want to launch legal proceedings," he stressed, with his love for concise, if also sometimes very simple, language, "and we won't try to figure out who was right and who was wrong. The responsibility is shared. Rather we say quite simply: "Let's get together and stop the quarrels!" A year before his election as pope, at a study week in Palermo on the problems of the Christian East, he had made unmistakably clear that the blame for the schism lay only in part at the door of the separated brethren, "*ma in gran parte è nostra*—most of it is ours."

A French Protestant magazine later called John XXIII the first pope to really hear what the Reformation was trying to say. The traditionalists in his Church still castigate him for that today. In the seminaries of archconservative Marcel Lefèbvre ten years after John's death the pictures of Pius XII were still hanging on the walls, as if time had stood still. As far as Catholic fundamentalists are concerned, the relativizing of truth, the dangerous blurring of the boundaries, began with Pope John. Cardinal Siri of Genua, who played an important role in both the 1978 papal elections as a candidate of the hard-liners, supposedly said that it would take the Church fifty years to recover from the mistakes made by this man.

It would be impossible to misread the profoundly conservative Roncalli more completely. He was a pope who more than once called priests to obedience with sharply worded strictures, who recommended "proceeding carefully" with social change, and who unmistakably declared at one audience: "In everyday life one often hears people say: the Church could be more lenient; it could accept a few minor concessions . . . Never! The pope can be kind and patient as much as you want; but, given the deplorable realities and the unacceptable omissions, his attitude will be, cost what it may, solid, clear, and unchangeable out of obedience to and respect for the faith."

In the year the Council opened, in a ceremony over the tomb of St. Peter, surrounded by all the Roman clergy, John solemnly signed the Apostolic Constitution *Veterum Sapientia* (Wisdom of the Ancients), which no one remembers anymore and which prescribed Latin as the language of instruction for all seminaries and Catholic faculties. In his bishop's household in Bergamo, he recalled, women were never mentioned, "as if there were no women in the world"—and he was still proud of it.

At a general audience in St. Peter's a Spanish woman stirred his ire when out of sheer enthusiasm over the pope, who was just then entering the cathedral, she lifted up her arms and began playing a pair of castanets. John bade the *sedia gestatoria* stop in front of the surprised woman, and gave her a dressing-down. Such clatter, he said, was out of place in God's house.

John didn't restrain the Holy Office when it put a halt to the "worker priest" experiment. He issued mistrustful briefs against overly free interpretation of the New Testament and dangerous tendencies in the work of Teilhard de Chardin (though a few days later he coolly declared that the warning about Teilhard was "regrettable"). Shortly before his death he refused to take several books off the Index, which was still in effect at the time.

The diocesan synod of Rome, held in 1960 for the first time since 1461, was considered a dry run for the Council—and it disappointed everyone. The almost 800 prepared resolutions were rushed through non-stop, without discussion. They dealt with such earthshaking issues as the soutane (priests had to wear it at all times), going to racetracks (forbidden for clerics), socializing with Freemasons (permissible only with great caution) and women (a priest should never drive a car with a woman passenger, even his sister). Meanwhile the great metropolis, whose population had quintupled in half a century, had long since become a mission territory (that was Pius XII's own term when he spoke to a gathering of Lenten preachers in Rome); and the deficits in pastoral care were especially glaring in the slums and shanty towns on the edge of Rome. But John XXIII was evidently so proud of "his" synod, that he thrust a copy of the just-published documentary volume about it into the hands of Archbishop Fisher of Canterbury when the latter visited him in the Vatican.

That, too, was John, the reform pope, a man who can't be easily pigeonholed in the party of progress, any more than he could when as Patriarch Roncalli of Venice he sent friendly greetings to the party congress of the Nenni Socialiasts and at the same time forbade his clergy to acquire TV sets. Priests who neglected their appearance were presented with a clean Roman collar from the patriarch.

Back when he was in France, the heartland of intellectually vital Catholicism, he showed little interest in the new theology; and he defended celibacy as vehemently as if belief in the Trinity were at stake. But the same Roncalli rehabilitated critical spirits like John Henry Newman and Antonio Rosmini. He called freedom a "daughter of God" and shielded German moral theologian Bernhard Häring from agents of the Holy Office.

In 1934, writing from Sofia, he had encouraged his father to discuss the painful problem of the cramped kitchen in the Colombera at a family council, whose only other members, apart from their mother, were the brother. "The women have to obey and not command!" he said. But three decades later in 1962 in his encyclopedia *Pacem in Terris* he was the first pope in history to pay tribute to the part played by women in public life and to the growing awareness of their human dignity.

The tradition-conscious, conservative priest Angelo Roncalli didn't become a renewer of the Church by doing a sudden about-face, but by always openly confronting his time. He was curious, ready to dialogue, capable of learning, not anxious and mistrustful. With the wisdom one acquires only from a long life's experience he never confused external discipline with inner strength.

Naturally there had to be obedience when the essentials of the Church were at stake. But that was something different from bowing and scraping before its functionaries. A young priest from abroad entered the Vatican, where he was visibly nervous about doing everything right. John is said to have calmed him: "My dear son, don't be so worried. You can be sure that at the Last Judgment Jesus won't ask you, 'And how did you make out with the Holy Office?'"

Fear of new ways and an uncertain future is a recurrent feature of church history. It leads many people to define the outer boundaries of the Church more clearly, to keep a sharper eye on unusual methods of pastoral care, and to insist on complete conformity with tradition. Pope John, too, valued tradition. However, he didn't want to take this treasure and bury it, but to make it fruitful for the present. That was his kind of revolution—- to throw all the antiquated stuff overboard and keep the essentials.

He was convinced that, "He who believes does not tremble" (a quotation from Isaiah 28:16; "He who believes will not be in haste" is a more modern translation). Roncalli's joy in human contact, his capacity for dialogue was no cheap way of currying favor. It came from his rock-solid faith, which gave him courage to approach dissenters openly and cordially. He insisted that, "We believe confidently that God is at work in the conscience of the individual person, that he is present in history"—because Christ has not left the world that he redeemed.

For this reason his encouragement is still valid today, decades later. Instead of issuing condemnations, one has to offer the world an attractive example. "Lamenting evil," John said, "makes people sad. Yet we know that complaints alone don't remove evil . . . Goodness has to be proclaimed!"

11

The Legacy

It is not the Gospel that changed. No, it is we who are just
beginning to understand it better.

—*Pope John XXIII*

THE POPE, WHO COULD LAUGH so light-heartedly, thought about
death all his life. In 1939 in Istanbul he made an entry in his diary
shortly before his fifty-eighth birthday, telling himself to look on
every extra year as a gift; his bishop, Radini-Tedeschi, had lived to be
only fifty seven. In 1947 while making his retreat in Paris he wrote:
"Having begun my sixty-seventh year of life, one has to be ready for
everything." In Venice in 1955: Whatever may be left of life "should
be nothing but a serenely cheerful preparation for death."

By the end of 1961 he was eighty years old, when he made the
rather casual remark in his diary: "I note in my body the beginning of
some kind of disturbance. At my age that is no doubt quite natural. I
bear it peacefully, even though it sometimes becomes bothersome,
also because I'm afraid it might get worse. It's not good to think too
much about it. But nonetheless I feel prepared for anything."

A year later, shortly before the opening of the Council, specialists
were called into the Vatican. The stomach troubles had worsened. John
had gotten weak and fatigued; his face was transparent like alabaster. In
November, after a severe hemorrhage, it was clear to the doctors that
the cancer, which had attacked so many members of his family had the
pope in its grip as well. "It's a tumor," his old friend and family physi-
cian Professor Gasbarrini from Bologna cautiously informed him.

He didn't tell the pope that it was an inoperable stomach can-

Marked by death: Pope John at
his last public appearance, at the
window of his apartment high
above St. Peter's Square on May
23, 1963, the feast of Ascension.
Courtesy Loris Capovilla, "L'ite
missa est di papa Giovanni"

cer, or that he had only half a year to live. Nonetheless John understood. "*Ebbene*, oh well, may God's will be done. Don't be worried
about me. My suitcases are packed. I'm ready to go."

His iron constitution kept the pope alive longer than expected,
but he was never without pain. He felt, "like St. Lawrence on the
gridiron," he once told his secretary.

Nevertheless he remained composed. He wrote loving farewell
letters to Sotto il Monte. He calmed his visitors, who had a lump in
their throats, telling them that everyone faces death sooner or later,
and the Church wouldn't go under because of him. "In a month
they get it done," he joked to the Polish Cardinal Wyszynski, "bury-
ing a pope and making a new one." His chamberlain Guido Gusso
asked him to bless his little son, and the three-year-old boy chirped,
perhaps out of politeness, that he wanted to be a priest like the
pope. John broke out into a hearty laugh and shook his head: "No,
you're too pretty. When the time comes, you'll get married!"

During Lent he again visited the parishes of Rome, plagued by
shortness of breath, but radiating more kindness than ever. In the
spring his devastated stomach refused to take nourishment; and
John had to be fed intravenously. There were more hemorrhages.
On May 22, 1963 he spoke for the last time to the crowds gathered
out on St. Peter's Square, painfully smiling but his voice still hearty:
"Happy Ascension Day! Let us hurry to the Lord, who goes up into
heaven. And if we cannot follow him and we remain on earth, let us
do what the apostles did, who gathered in the hall of the Lord's
Supper and prayed for the Holy Spirit. . . . *Saluti, Saluti!*"

On the night of May 30 he had a bad hemorrhage. Then peri-
tonitis; the tumor broke through his intestinal wall and spread its
poison throughout his body. The doctor told him that the end was
near—and again the pope smiled. "I'm ready." Capovilla broke
down crying next to the bed. John stroked his hair and said with a
gentle reproach, "I'm a bishop and I have to die this way, simply, but
with dignity, and you have to help me."

Cardinals, doctors, the nuns from the papal household streamed
into the dying man's room. John XXIII sat upright in bed and
pointed to the crucifix on the wall that met his eye when he woke
up and before he fell asleep. "Look there, these open arms have

been the program of my time in office. They say that Christ died for everyone, for one and all. No one is excluded from his love, his forgiveness. . . . Everybody helped me and loved me, I received a lot of encouragement. I'm not aware that I offended anyone; but if I did, I ask for forgiveness . . . In this last hour I feel peaceful and sure that the Lord in his grace will not reject me. . . . My time draws near to its end, but Christ lives on, and the Church continues its work . . . *Ut unum sint, ut unum sint!* That all may be one!"

In the evening Montini arrived, the man he had meanwhile named a cardinal and rather openly presented as his crown prince, along with his sister and brothers, Assunta, Alfredo, Giuseppe, and Zaverio. They watched and prayed near his bed. At night the pope stayed awake, became confused, broke into French, believed he was in France, and that his Parisian doctor was standing by his side. Then he recognized his family, drank a cup of coffee, and declared in merry surprise, "I'm still here! Yesterday I thought I'd be already gone . . ."

This death agony lasted eighty-three hours, and the whole world took part in it. The Vatican Press Agency issued hourly medical bulletins. Telegrams arrived from every corner of the world, letters from American children—"Dear Pope John, we love you"—from Protestants, Buddhists, Jews, unbelievers ("Insofar as an atheist can pray, I'm praying for you"), from Kennedy, De Gaulle, Queen Elizabeth, Fidel Castro in Cuba, and Kremlin chief Khrushchev, from the inmates of the Regina Coeli prison, who had not forgotten his Christmas visit. In the cathedral of Milan 20,000 young people prayed an entire night for the dying pope. In the synagogue of Rome Chief Rabbi Eliseo Toaf recited psalms for his health. The traditional parade on Italy's national holiday was cancelled to spare the mortally ill man the sound of jet fighters.

John XXIII lay beneath an oxygen mask and could breathe only with difficulty. He had fits of fever and kept losing consciousness. His pulse would improve for a short time and he would converse with his siblings—in the Bergamask dialect—continually repeating words from the Gospels, "I am the resurrection and the life!"

On Pentecost Sunday June 2, tens of thousands of Romans, pilgrims, and tourists gathered out on St. Peter's Square. They looked up in silence to the rooms on fourth floor of the Apostolic Palace.

The pope followed the mass in his study which was next to his bedroom, but could no longer receive communion. His fever rose, his pulse accelerated, his breathing was labored, but John was fully conscious. In the evening the communiqué from the Vatican Press Agency contained only a single word: *Gravissimo*—extremely bad.

But the powerful nature of the peasant's son managed to fight back the killing disease for one more night. "The Holy Father is suffering terribly," explained a Vatican spokesman to the 250 waiting journalists, "and he knows how to suffer." Minutes of merciful unconsciousness gave way to long phases of piercing pain, blood transfusions, doses of oxygen. "Stop crying," John abruptly told his sister and brothers. "Pentecost is a day of joy!"

On the evening of Whitmonday, June 3, 1963, around 7 o'clock Cardinal Luigi Traghlia, the pope's deputy in the episcopate of Rome, began to celebrate mass out on St. Peter's Square. An immense crowd of people filled the broad circle; many people were kneeling on the warm stones, staring through their tears at the windows behind which the pope laid wrestling with death.

His nephew Don Battista would later report that John could no longer speak, but moved his head and made weak signs with his hands until those present understood. At one point his brother Zaverio was standing in front of the bed in such a way that he was unintentionally covering up the crucifix on the opposite wall. He immediately stepped aside, and a happy smile spread over the emaciated face of the pope when he could once again see Christ.

At the moment when the mass came to an end, and Cardinal Traghlia spoke the old formula of dismissal, *Ite, missa est*, the light was switched on in the darkened bedroom on the fourth floor. On St. Peter's Square the people began to weep uncontrollably, as they fell into each other's arms: John was dead.

"In the hour when we say farewell, or rather, till we meet again," writes Roncalli at the end of his Spiritual Testament, composed in Venice in 1954, "I think back once more to what counts the most in life: Jesus Christ, his holy Church, his Gospel, and in the Gospel above all the 'Our Father' in the spirit and according to the Heart of Jesus, and from the Gospel: the truth and the kindness, the mild and benign, the active and patient, the unconquerable and victorious kindness."

The memory of the loving kindness of God, which he embodied, will remain. Perhaps, too, a bit of courage for the "holy craziness," which according to one of his countless bons mots is part of the Church. He was reluctant to speak *ex cathedra* and lay claim to infallibility, which was something the modern world would never understand, but which would also not have matched his image of the Petrine office.

The open doors will remain open—the readiness to work together with people who have different beliefs and "all men and women of good will," as he says in his encyclical on peace. A new sensitivity to the Jewish roots of Christianity will remain. We know how when he was in Istanbul, he tried to help those persecuted by the Nazis. In Paris he had a crowd of Jewish friends. In a sermon in the cathedral of Algiers he called the Jews "sons of the promise" and Abraham "the patriarch of all believers."

Then years later, 200 delegates from the American United Jewish Appeal visited the Vatican. Pope John came up to them with arms wide open and quoted—alluding to his second name, Giuseppe—the famous line from the Bible: "I am Joseph, your brother!"

A scene that took place at the Good Friday liturgy in 1962 at St. Peter's caused a worldwide stir: during the "Great Litanies," which precede the veneration of the Cross, a cardinal, probably out of old habit, sang the traditional formula, *Oremus et pro perfidis Judaeis*— "Let us also pray for the faithless Jews: God, you do not exclude even the faithless Jews from your mercy. Hear our prayers, which we bring before you because of the blinding of that people . . ." At this point the pope interrupted the service and rebuked the wearer of the purple: "Repeat the petition—but use the new form!"

This was because back in 1959, on the first Good Friday of his papacy, John had replaced those harsh words with a prayer text that was not only friendlier in its language, but theologically correct. Since then it has been used throughout the Church: "Let us pray also for the Jews, to whom God, our Lord, first spoke. May he keep them in fidelity to his covenant and in the love of his name, so that they may reach the goal to which his will wishes to lead them." Pope Pius XII had already begun to reform the embarrassing rite by allowing the term "faithless" to be replaced by "unbelieving." He also prescribed kneeling down at this point, which was usual with all the other Good Friday petitions and was omitted only at the "prayer for the Jews" out of contempt.

The encouragement will remain that John gave for tackling social problems and for giving the poor of the industrial metropolises and the Third World something more than speeches full of pity. Roncalli's social encyclical *Mater et Magistra* (Mother and Teacher, meaning the Church) rates in-house decision-making and shared ownership of companies by their workers among the elementary demands of justice. Economic progress must be followed up by social progress, "so that all groups of the population can participate appropriately in the growing wealth of the nation."

What is new here is the worldwide perspective of this teaching, which demands an active solidarity of the industrial nations with the countries living in wretched poverty, which rejects economic aid linked to political influence as a "new form of colonialism," and which challenges the Christian world, as "the Church of the poor," to make its contribution to the balancing out of international interests.

Finally, his passionate protest over the arms race and war will remain. He had already warned in his first encyclical, that "too many soldiers' cemeteries blanket the earth." When German federal chancellor Konrad Adenauer visited the Vatican in 1960, he was hoping to come away with a few favorable words about rearming West German. As if he were out on the stump, he lectured Roncalli, who was listening amicably: "I believe that God has entrusted the German people in these times of need with the special task of being the guardian of the West against the powerful influences of the East, which weigh us down." John passed over this clumsy hint with a pregnant silence.

But years later at a reception for the bishops of Poland he praised Polish efforts to preserve the inviolability of borders—much to the irritation of Adenauer, whose government never recognized the Oder-Neisse line between Poland and Germany. "The world is poisoned by an unhealthy nationalism," Roncalli had noted in his diary when war broke out in 1939.

"Was Adenauer a Christian?" papal secretary Loris Capovilla asked a nonplussed German journalist Luitpold A. Dorn during an interview. When Dorn asked why Adenauer rejected Pope John,

Capovilla replied, "Because he considered him politically stupid."

Needless to say, John wasn't blind. He obviously knew about the priests incarcerated by the Communist regimes, about the destroyed churches, and the reprisals against people who dared, despite government bans on believing in God, to have a religious conscience and to talk about the Gospel. All of this caused him terrible suffering. In the presence of cardinals, seminarians and visitors at papal audiences he complained more than once about the suppression of religious freedom and the Church, for example, in Cuba and the Soviet Union.

But who derived any benefit from outraged condemnations? John thought he could more effectively help the persecuted Christians in the underground and better serve the cause of the faith behind the Iron Curtain if he strove to engage Communist rulers in dialogue, if he tried to understand their motives, whatever they might be, and offered respectful cooperation in the interests of humanity and social justice.

When he took office as pope, John faced an explosive political situation, with an icy atmosphere prevailing between the power blocs, powerless international organizations (the UN was only thirteen years old) and an arms race that might lead at any moment to an exchange of nuclear strikes with unforeseeable consequences for the entire world. In John's view the Church was better off promoting the first hesitant steps toward dialogue, openness and reconciliation, instead of pouring more fuel on the fire through partisanship and strong language. He had explicitly charged the work group that composed *Pacem in terris* to his specifications to dispense with condemnations of communism: "I cannot ascribe bad will to the one or the other side. If I do that, then there will be no dialogue, and all the doors will slam shut."

Diplomat Roncalli, who was still greatly deficient in smoothness and cunning, but for all that a consummate professional, changed the Vatican's habits gently and tenaciously. Only rarely did word of his new approach leak out and prompt heated discussion about the new *Ostpolitik* on the Tiber. "The Russians are wonderful people," he remarked in a private conversation,

We shouldn't condemn them just because we have problems with their political system. They have a great, intact spiritual legacy. We have to engage in dialogue—even today. We have to keep on trying to address the good that is in every person. Otherwise we could lose everything, if people don't find ways and means to work together to save peace. I have no fear about talking with each and everyone about peace on earth. If Khrushchev were sitting right where you are, I don't think I'd feel inhibited or uncomfortable about talking with him.

The piquant thing about all this is that Roncalli's conversation partner just then was the American journalist Norman Cousins, a gray eminence of international politics, the founder of the so-called "Dartmouth Group," which brought together high-ranking advisers of Kennedy and Khrushchev for informal discussions. Naturally the Kremlin chief heard about the pope's friendly words. He didn't turn down the medal blessed by John that Cousins passed on to him.

These signals flying back and forth between Rome and Moscow were not the first. There had been top-secret meetings in Roman apartments, encounters between Italian Catholics who had some grasp of the Italian Communists' desire for justice and Communists who believed in the poor Christ. One participant in these discussions was Palmiro Togliatti, secretary of the *Partito communista italiano*, who was just then preparing to travel to Moscow. He brought along with him the pope's discreet wish for a congratulatory telegram from the Kremlin on his upcoming eightieth birthday. *Il bravo signore*, the "good gentleman" in Moscow, had nothing to lose by it, because congratulating an eighty-year-old was everywhere considered an obvious act of politeness.

Nikita Sergeyevich Khrushchev laughed and drew up the telegram, which arrived punctually on November 25, 1961 at noon at the residence of the Soviet ambassador in Rome. He took the unusual document to the papal nuncio in Italy, who passed it on to the Secretariat of State. John was glad: "Something is moving in the world." He made a remark about a "sign from Providence" and disappeared into his private chapel, leaving everyone there in helpless confusion. How were they to react to it without coming under suspicion of being henchmen of communism? They handed the pope their proposed response: a few skimpy set phrases, but he scratched them all out—as he liked to do—and sent "the entire Russian nation" his "hearty wishes for the development and strengthening of universal peace through hopeful understanding in humanity and brotherliness."

The chemistry was just right between the two peasant's sons with their somewhat coarse exterior and their down-to-earth way of thinking. Khrushchev's daughter Rada later said after her audience with the pope that his hands were tanned like her father's by hard farm work. And it should not be forgotten that despite his tyrannical behavior Khrushchev was driven by some liberal visions, and he was having difficulties with the cementheads in the Kremlin like those John was having with some curial prelates.

"By the very fact that he acted like a simple pastor, he inspired confidence," is the judgment of historian and journalist Hansjakob Stehle, a long-time authority on relations between the Vatican and Eastern Europe, "and he kept the initial contact safely removed from the obstacles of prestige and protocol. Thirty-five years after the last discussions by Eugenio Pacelli with the Soviets, this was the only method that could have opened the way to large-scale church diplomacy."

And to the new freedoms. Up until just before the opening of the Council it had looked as if no observers from the Russian Orthodox Church would take part in the gathering. Western politics, the newspaper of the Moscow patriarchate intoned, would only exploit the Council as an "ideological weapon" against the Soviet Union. Then suddenly a thaw set in among the Kremlin and Russian orthodox leadership; and on October 12, 1962, one day after the Council started, Archpriest Vitaly Brovoy and Archimandrite Vladimir Kotliarov caused a sensation by arriving in Rome as official envoys of the Holy Synod.

"We want no protection and no special privileges," John informed the Soviet chief of state, "we simply want freedom to preach the Gospel." Could this innocent request still be met with Stalin's scornful "How many divisions does the pope have?" Besides, the Kremlin needed to score a few public relations points, because it wished to intensify its economic ties with the West, and in the face of growing tensions with China it couldn't really wage the Cold War anymore.

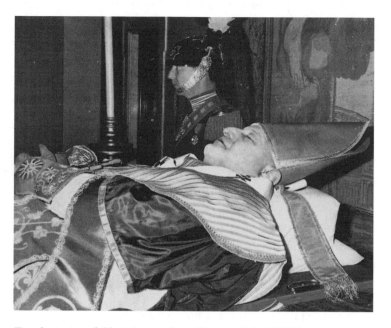

For the unity of Christians and world peace John XXIII
wished to sacrifice his life on a long, painful path to
death: the pope, who died on June 3, 1963, laid out in
St. Peter's. *Courtesy* Giordani

The new relationship between Rome and Moscow passed the first acid test during the Cuban missile crisis of October, 1962. Here John XXIII played the role of a non-partisan mediator between the superpowers, presumably making a crucial contribution to the prevention of a nuclear war. The Soviets had begun to set up rocket bases capable of reaching the USA. The Americans met this threat with a naval blockade of Soviet ships supplying rocket materials to Cuba. In Washington the evacuation of politicians' families had begun. American B-52 bombers were already airborne so that in case of a sudden escalation Moscow, Leningrad and Kiev could be turned into smoldering ruins. The situation was a powder keg with the fuse already lit.

While the hard-liners in the Pentagon flexed their muscles, JFK, a Catholic, aimed at limiting the conflict. He gave the USSR an ultimatum—withdraw the ships or be attacked—but at the same time sent his brother Bobby to Soviet ambassador Anatoly Dobrinin (the two understood one another surprisingly well), and had Norman Cousins feel out the Vatican. The Flemish Dominican priest Félix Morlion, who had once worked in the curia and was now thought to be a CIA agent, joined in the conference calls. Soviet writers and scholars were brought in too.

In the end it was clear that a call for peace from the pope would be the readiest way for both sides to pull back honorably without loss of face. On the night of October 25 the pope was awakened, a message to the superpowers was composed, its text translated immediately into Russian and English, and dispatched to both the White House and the Kremlin. By 7 a.m., a positive answer had come from Moscow; an hour later Kennedy, too, gave the green light. At noon John XXIII read his message over the radio microphone.

The pope spoke in French: "With my hand on my heart," John begged the leaders of the superpowers, "may they hear the cry of fear that rises up to heaven from all parts of the world, from the innocent children to the old people, from individuals to communities: Peace, Peace!" On October 26 *Pravda*'s banner headlines covered the entire first page with a quotation from the pope: "We ask the rulers not to be deaf to the cry of humanity."

On October 28 Nikita Khrushchev ordered the dismantling of

the rocket bases and the commencement of negotiations through the UN. The ships had already turned around. Politically speaking, Moscow had been forced to back down, but morally speaking, Khrushchev had made an incalculable gain: he now had the image of a friend of peace prepared to make sacrifices. According to Andreotti, the pope sent a cable to Kennedy. "Don't bask in the victory!" JFK replied, "I wouldn't dream of it."

In a kind of critical rehash of the maneuver the papal peace initiative came up once again on December 13, 1962 in Khrushchev's study, when the mysterious Norman Cousins sat with the Russian for more than three hours. Afterwards the Vatican Secretariat of State received a twenty-page report. Khrushchev said he was grateful to the pope, but didn't want to convert him: "I myself was religious in my youth. Stalin was even in a seminary. . . . What we were fighting against back then wasn't religion as such, but a special situation in which a lot of politics was involved . . ."

He wanted to have long-term lines (unofficial ones, of course) of communication to the Vatican. He acknowledged the efforts of the Vatican to serve all men and women, because it was dedicated to the higher values of life. Then Cousins carefully, but plainly raised the issue of reprisals against religion: religious instruction, religious literature, the Ukrainian Metropolitan Slipyi, who was still living in Siberian exile. Khrushchev took notes, growled something about "having it looked into," but then with sudden candor went into the Slipyi problem. "If there's a guarantee that they won't make a political case out of it," he could imagine Slipyi being released, even if though tongues would wag. "One enemy more at liberty doesn't worry me . . ."

Josyf Slipyi was the metropolitan of Ukrainian Eastern-rite Catholics whom Stalin had driven into the underground. He had spent seventeen years in Soviet prisons and penal camps, where word was that he had also been tortured. As a matter of fact, two months later the broken old man was allowed to leave Siberia. Jan Willebrands, Cardinal Bea's closest associate in the Secretariat for the Unity of Christians picked him up in Moscow, and after discussions lasting for days talked him out of his wish to visit his Ukrainian home. "Political" sensation had to be avoided at all costs.

The prominent ex-prisoner was allowed only to take a train that passed through his episcopal city Lviv (Lemberg) to Vienna and Rome. From the window of the express train he blessed Lviv and all of the Ukraine unobserved. At the last station before Rome, in Orte, Slipyi and Willebrands got out to dodge any journalists who might be waiting in ambush at the end of the line. From Orte he was taken by Capovilla to the Vatican. There an emotionally charged pope was already waiting; he warmly embraced the metropolitan and greeted him as "my lord cardinal"—an honor that he actually got from Paul VI, since John died before the planned consistory. Slipyi lived for another twenty years secluded in the Vatican, and died at the age of ninety-two.

Shortly after this, without much publicity, the papal under-secretary of state, Agostino Casaroli (under Paul VI he would become the definitive architect of a new Vatican *Ostpolitik*) managed to free four Hungarian bishops who had been exiled far from their dioceses. Of course, the Hungarian primate Cardinal József Mindszenty remained stuck in the American Embassy in Budapest. And the archbishop of Prague, Josef Beran, who for sixteen years had not been allowed to set foot in his official residence on the Hradschin, was not released from internment until 1965—at the price of emigrating to Rome.

A few weeks after Slipyi's release came a spectacular visit to the Vatican from Khrushchev's son-in-law Alexei Adzhubey. At the time Adzhubey was one of the most powerful men in the Kremlin; as editor-in-chief of the official government organ *Izvestia* he could justify his presence to the hawks in his own camp by claiming that he just wanted to interview the pope. John ran into similar resistance: how could he grant the honor of an audience to a declared atheist, the representative of a bloodstained regime that persecuted Christians?

Once again John couldn't understand what all the fuss was about. "An atheist?" he smiled. "Now in the worst case what can he say to me? That the Church is finished, that it's dead. Good, but I'll tell him it isn't true."

"The people around me are not very enthusiastic about my having received someone from the Soviet Union," he confided to the cardinal of Paris, François Marty, after the visit ended. "But all my life I've gotten used to opening my door to whoever knocks." John knew that some people in the curia and among Italian Catholic right-wingers took him to be a political dimwit, whose friendly gestures were simply giving ammunition to red propaganda while carelessly ignoring the danger of communism. The pope, it is said, told the editor-in-chief of the Jesuit journal *Civiltà Cattolica* that he had to be very careful, "so that the next conclave isn't a conclave against me and doesn't elect someone to destroy everything I tried to achieve."

Perhaps he also knew that the KGB had planted spies in the Vatican—as Russian historian Valery Arkadevich Alekseyev, Khrushchev's man in charge of relations with the Vatican, later revealed. And he may have known that conversely the CIA was using the shady Father Morlion to keep an eye on the contacts between Norman Cousins and the Kremlin.

On March 7, 1963 Adzhubey was led past a crowd of gaping colleagues and photographers into the pope's private library. John himself had only three months to live. It was the first meeting of a high Soviet official with the pope since the Russian Revolution of 1917. Adzhubey had brought his wife, Rada Khrushcheva, the daughter of the Kremlin chief, who understood French. John took the opportunity to tell her stories in French about the paintings and tapestries in the library. With her husband he went into raptures about Slavic music and his fond memories of Bulgaria. He reaffirmed that the pope saw all people as brothers—and suddenly the devout atheist Adzhubey found himself in a religious conversation with the leader of world Catholicism.

"You are a journalist," the pope beamed at him, "so of course you know the Bible and the story of creation." Nobody could be at once so single-minded and so unobtrusive as John the magician. "The Bible tells us that God created the world, and the light on the first day. But, you know, the Bible's days are really epochs, and these epochs last a very long time." And now John got to the point: "We look one another in the eye, and we see a light. Today is the first day of creation, the day of light. Everything takes time. The light is in my eyes and in your eyes. If God wills, he will show us a way."

In the end John put on his most entrancing smile, took Rada's hand tenderly in his, and asked, "What are your children's names? There's something unique about a mother saying the names of her children." Rada answered proudly, "Nikita, Alexey, Ivan." Those were rather foreign-sounding names for the halls the Vatican, but John was in his element; he knew the relevant patron saints from his time in the East and told the mother about their legends. He especially liked the name of the youngest—the Russian equivalent of John, Giovanni. His father and his grandfather had been called John. "Ivan, Ivan, that's what I'd be, I who liked being called John. I have such a special liking . . . for John the Baptist and John the Evangelist, that after my election as pope I asked them to accompany me as guardian angels during my pontificate. When you go home, Madame, bring a tender greeting to Ivan; the other two won't hold it against me."

That, too, was a way of doing politics, by casting seed corns of humanity into the furrows of a frozen field.

After the audience Adzhubey spoke with a reporter from the right-wing weekly *Il Tempo*: "This is a man of great and genuine simplicity," he said. "You turn your eyes to him, you look at him, and you immediately feel great respect and at the same time a sudden trust in him."

But the encounter in the pope's library, which reads like a romance, had a terrible flip side: Valery Alekseyev claims that enemies of dialogue in the KGB tried to assassinate Adzhubey and disguise it as an auto accident. Khrushchev's son-in-law, however, got word of the plan and changed cars. The victim of the attack turned out to be a correspondent for *Izvestia*, who ironically had been in the service of the KGB.

As part of the Adzhubey visit it was also announced that the pope was to receive the peace prize of the International Balzan Foundation. In the Secretariat of State critical voices were raised: it wasn't proper for a pope to accept a prize and to compete with others for an award that belonged to his office as a successor of St. Peter.

John XXIII was unimpressed by such complaints. For his encyclical *Pacem in terris* (Peace on Earth), which he himself thought of as his legacy, he was ready to enlist any kind of publicity. Published on April 11, 1963, *Pacem in terris* was the first encyclical aimed not just at bishops, clerics, and Catholic lay people, but explicitly addressed "to all men of good will."

This deeply moving testament by a doomed man argues that lasting peace is dependent upon a just world order; it argues for mutual trust and honest treaties; it sees elementary human rights — including those of minorities—as grounded in the Gospel. John speaks not only of the Church's right to proclaim its faith freely and without hindrance, as had been usual hitherto; he also speaks very clearly about the right of every person to worship God according to his or her conscience, about the right of the so-called developing countries to decide their own future.

In the characteristic emancipation movements of the modern world—the social ascent of the working class, the participation of women in public life, the political independence of peoples formerly ruled by others—John XXIII sees the Holy Spirit wafting through history. Catholics should cooperate with this and work together with non-Catholics whenever it served the public good.

There had been popes before John who fought passionately for peace, men like Benedict XV, whose heart was broken by the sight of nations butchering one another in World War One. But Roncalli was the first pope to proscribe the bloodbath of war as criminal. He could no longer imagine a "just war." He didn't believe in the arms build-up or the value of nuclear weapons as a deterrent, and he shared the conviction of many people that in the nuclear age war had ceased to be an appropriate means of restoring violated rights. Differences between nations should be settled through treaties and negotiation, not by armed violence.

John XXIII writes: "Hence justice, sound reason and the feeling for human dignity demand that the worldwide arms race should stop; furthermore, that the weapons that are already available in various countries be mutually and simultaneously reduced, and finally that an effective, reciprocal disarmament be agreed on." Peace couldn't really be secured merely by a fragile military equilibrium, "but through mutual trust" and the "laws of sound reason."

This time the reviews were mixed. "Utopian dreams," snorted *The New York Times*, noting that John's proposals for disarmament ran counter to American policy. The UN General Assembly, on the other hand, had Cardinal Suenens explain the encyclical and posed many interesting questions—John had counted the existence of the UN and its 1948 Universal Declaration of Human Rights as one of divinely wrought "signs of the times."

At the end of April the right-wing Italian press was in an uproar after the Communists gained more than a million more votes in the parliamentary elections. Needless to say, it blamed John with his audience for the Khrushchev family and his naive peace encyclical. Didn't he sympathize with the controversial Aldo Moro, who dreamt of an *apertura a sinistra*, an opening of his Christian Democratic party to the left, indeed of alliances with the Socialists? Hadn't Cardinal Ottaviani warned high-ranking military figures that the audience with Adzhubey and the "introduction of the distinction between mistakes and the people making them" in *Pacem in terris* would have the direst consequences? A Milan newspaper furiously called the encyclical *Falcem in terris*, "sickle on earth," alluding to the communist symbol.

There were also appalled commentaries in the conservative German media. Others in the press were enthusiastic: *Time-Life* invited Pope John, Kennedy, Khrushchev, Adenauer, de Gaulle, Pablo Picasso, and Swiss theologian Karl Barth (all of whom had been featured on the cover of *Time*) to a summit dinner in New York. John supposedly did not flatly reject the notion; that sort of idea, he thought, needed time to ripen.

The pope never got to hear the sound of the largest bells in Taizé, which the French ecumenical community christened *Pacem in terris*, nor the choral symphony *Pacem in terris*, which Darius Milhaud, a Jew, composed for the dedication of the new Parisian radio building: but John had written the only encyclical set to music in the history of Christianity.

On May 1 John had only four more weeks to live. With his shriveled up face and his tired, lackluster eyes he looked like someone from another world, as an American monsignor introduced him to John McCone from the Secret Service. McCone warned the pope about the wily Kremlin chief and the not quite so wily Italian communists, but he was wasting his breath. "I will not change my style on account of the impertinent fuss with which such people are trying to intimidate men of the Church," John declared in an unusually frosty tone. "My blessing goes out to all nations, and I withhold my trust from no one."

Two weeks later President Kennedy, the Catholic in the White House, comforted the pope. Through Cardinal Richard Cushing of

Boston he sent word, "that the government of the United States regrets and considers unfounded the suggestions that are being heard in the press and in certain political circles." People in the Vatican Secretariat of State were not so understanding: Monsignor dell'Acqua and other heavyweights stopped *L'Osservatore Romano*, Radio Vatican and other official church media from publishing any details of the conversation with Adzhubey, as the pope had wished, in order to head off the escalating speculation about concessions or imminent political alliances.

If the usually very well-informed Vatican insider Giancarlo Zizola is right, John complained bitterly about this obstructionist policy: the "unconditional clarity" of his remarks deserved

> to be made known and not withheld under some pretense. It should be clearly stated that the pope does not need to defend himself. . . . But the first section [of the Secretariat of State] doesn't agree, and I don't like that one bit. It's what the pope wants! . . . I lament and pity those who in the last few days have let themselves by carried away into engaging in unspeakable little tricks.

It was probably the same forces who in November, 1964 and once again in October, 1965 joined in horror-struck resistance to the proposal of some bishops that the Council canonize John XXIII by acclamation, as had occasionally been done at synods over the course of church history. For one thing, people were unwilling to discredit by that sort of spontaneous action the very meticulous "trial," which had meantime begun, that precedes a beatification or canonization and that investigates the candidate's life down to the last nook and cranny. For another thing, influential circles in the curia were afraid that the "Roncalli line," which they had rejected, might be ennobled by the acclamation in a way that would make it an unquestionable norm.

Fortunately the beatification did take place on Sept. 3, 2000, but characteristically Angelo Roncalli was beatified in a "package deal" with the completely different Pius IX. Pio Nono had ruled from 1846 to 1878. He was a skilled pastoral practitioner, who first came on the scene bearing hopes for opening up the Church, but then under the pressure of political developments turned into a narrow-minded cultural warrior. His *Syllabus of Errors* (1864) condemned "progress, liberalism and modern civilization" in 80 detailed anathemas. Modern church historians also criticize him for ordering the kidnapping and baptism of Jewish children.

Nevertheless, the Church will never again be able to abandon the path that Pope John "so masterfully traced out for the future," as Cardinal Montini put it, a few days before becoming his successor. He had, Montini wrote in an obituary in the *Corriere della Sera*, "given the Church a deeper awareness of herself and of the mission that Christ continues in her," and "awakened [in her bosom] enormous spiritual energies that make her appear vital and young."

When Roncalli's legacy is mentioned, people usually cite his deeply pious, but somewhat conventional-sounding Spiritual Testament of 1954. But there is another legacy that looks far ahead into the future, a simple stock-taking of his life and at the same time a rousing vision of the Church.

In the last days of May, 1963 John felt that his life was coming to an end. He was dead-tired, was being given intravenous feedings, blood and plasma transfusions. On the feast of the Ascension he showed himself to the people out on St. Peter's Square for the last time. The next day he gathered his closest coworkers about him—his secretary Loris Capovilla, Monsignor dell'Acqua from the Secretariat of State, Cardinal Amleto Cicognani, the senior member of the College of Cardinals—sat up in bed and solemnly declared that with death approaching he wished to renew his faith.

That was how priests liked to do it, at least in Italy. When it came time to die, they looked back over their life, recalled the early awakening of their love for Jesus, came before Jesus, who was soon to be their judge, and said: for all my weaknesses and mistakes I have tried to remain true to you; be true to me now, cover with your mercy whatever was false and bad in me, and take me to your Paradise.

John had repeatedly prayed that way, examining his conscience, renewing his trust in God's forgiving goodness, as the *Giornale dell'Anima* attests. But what he now said to his coworkers sounded different. Untroubled by the fact that they hadn't always followed him, he once again explained to them the motives for his action, his yearning for freedom, his love for human beings. For one last time he showed how he wished to be understood and remembered.

Capovilla recorded this unusual legacy: "In the presence of my coworkers," John said, "it spontaneously comes to my mind to renew the act of faith. This is fitting for us priests to do, for we have to deal with the things of heaven for the welfare of the entire world; and hence we have to let ourselves be guided by the will of God. Today more than ever, and certainly more than in the last few centuries, we are oriented to serving humanity as such, not just Catholics, to defending first of all and everywhere the rights of the human person and not just those of the Catholic Church."

"Today's situation," John continues,

the challenges of the last fifty years and a more profound understanding of the faith have brought us face to face with new realities, as I said in my inaugural address to the Council. It is not the Gospel that has changed. No, we are the ones who are just now beginning to understand it better. Anyone who has lived a fairly long life, anyone who at the beginning of this century confronted the challenges of a social activity that dealt with the entire person, anyone who, like me, spent twenty years in the East and eight in France and by so doing could compare different cultures with one another, such a person knows that the moment has come to recognize the signs of the time, to seize the possibilities they offer and to look far ahead.

It was the testament of a prophet, a prophet like Moses, who had led a lazy, stiff-necked people, still longing to go back to their slaves' existence, into a better future, and who now as he died on Mount Nebo could see the Promised Land.

CHRONOLOGY

1881	Nov. 25: Angelo Roncalli is born to a sharecropper family in Sotto il Monte, Lombardy
1892–1900	In the minor and major seminary of Bergamo
1901–1905	Theological studies in Bergamo
1901–1902	Military service in the 73rd Infantry Regiment, Bergamo
1904	Oct. 8: Ordained a priest in Rome
1905–1914	Secretary of Bishop Giacomo Maria Radini-Tedeschi in Bergamo, docent for church history and patrology, newspaper editor, spiritual adviser to the Catholic Women's Association
1915–1918	Director of a student residence and spiritual father at the major seminary in Bergamo
1921–1924	President of the Advisory Board of the Papal Missions of Italy at the Vatican Congregation for Spreading the Faith (*Propaganda Fide*)
1924	Nov.: Professor of patrology at the Lateran University
1925	Mar. 19: Consecration as bishop in Rome
1925–1934	Apostolic Visitator, later Apostolic Delegate in Bulgaria. Official residence: Sofia
1935–1944	Apostolic delegate in Turkey and in Greece Official residence: Istanbul
1945–1952	Papal nuncio in Paris

1881 Freedom of press established in France
Vatican archives opened to scholars
Political parties founded in Japan
1892 First automatic telephone switchboard introduced
1901 Ragtime jazz develops in U.S.
1902 Enrico Caruso makes his first phonograph recording

1904 Church and state separated in France
1906 Pres. Theodore Roosevelt on first trip outside U.S. by a
president in office, visits canal zone
1909 Marks beginning of Plastic Age
1913 Balkan Wars
1915 Henry Ford develops farm tractor
First transcontinental telephone call
1921 Britain and Ireland sign peace treaty
Hitler's storm troopers (SA) begin to terrorize political
opponents
1922 Soviet states form U.S.S.R.
1924 First elections in Italy under fascists methods; 65 per cent
favor Mussolini

1935 Oil pipelines between Iraq, Haifa, and Tripolis opened
1940 World War II
Penicillin developed as a practical antibiotic
1945 "V.E. Day" ends war in Europe May 8
1949 Israel admitted to UN; capital moved from Tel Aviv to
Jerusalem
1950 25 Protestant and four Eastern Orthodox Church groups
organize National Council of the Curch of Christ in the
U.S.: 32 million members

1953	Dec. 1: Named a cardinal
1953–1958	Patriarch of Venice
1958	Oct. 9: Pius XII dies
	Oct. 28: Roncalli is elected pope
	Nov. 4: Coronation in St. Peter's
1958–1963	Pontificate of John XXIII
1959	Jan. 25: Announcement of the Second Vatican Council
1961	May 15: Social encyclopedia *Mater et Magistra*
1962	Oct. 11: Opening of Vatican II in St. Peter's
1963	Apr. 11: Peace encyclical *Pacem in terris*
	June 3: John XXIII dies at the age of 81
	June 6: Interment in the Vatican Grottos
2000	Sept. 3: Beatification

1953   Simon de Beauvoir: "The Second Sex"

1955   U.S.S.R. decrees end of war with Germany
       Automically generated power first used in U.S.
1958   U.S. launches first moon rocket
       Supreme Religious Center for World Jewry dedicated in
       Jerusalem
       The "Beatnik" movement, originating in California, spreads
       throughout America and Europe
1960   First weather satellite launched by U.S. to transmit TV
       images of cloud cover around the world

1963   U.S. President John F. Kennedy assassinated
       Major religions: 890 million Christians; 365 million
       Hindus; 200 million Buddhists; 13 million Jews
2000   Italian Jews denounce Vatican's decision to beatify Pius
       IX; further controversy surrounding beatification of Pius
       XII

Pius IX (Giovanni Mastai-Ferretti)	1846–1878
Leo XIII (Gioacchino Count Pecci):	1878–1903
Pius X (Giuseppe Sarto)	1903–1914
Benedict XV (Giacomo della Chiesa)	1914–1922
Pius XI (Achille Ratti)	1922–1939
Pius XII (Eugenio Pacelli)	1939–1958
John XXIII (Angelo Giuseppe Roncalli)	1958–1963
Paul VI (Giovanni Battista Montini)	1963–1978
John Paul I (Albino Luciani)	6/8/78–9/28/78
John Paul II (Karol Wojtyla)	10/16/78–

BIBLIOGRAPHY

Discorsi, Messaggi, Colloqui del Santo Padre Giovanni XIII. 6 vols. Vatican City, 1960–1967.

Giovanni XIII. *Il cardinale Cesare Baronio.* Rome, 1961

_____. *Il Giornale dell'Anima e altri scritti di pietà.* Rome, 1964.

_____. *Lettere 1958–1963*, ed. Loris Capovilla. Rome, 1978.

_____. *Lettere ai familiari.* Rome, 1968.

_____. *Erinnerungen eines Nuntius.* Freiburg im Breisgau, 1965.

Alberigo, Angelina and Giuseppe. *Giovanni XIII. Profezia nella fedeltà* (Dipartimento di scienze religiose 10). Brescia, 1978.

Alberigo, Giuseppe; Wittstadt, Klaus, eds. *Ein Blick zurück-nach vorn: Johannes XIII. Spiritualität—Theologie—Wirken (Studien zur Kirchengeschichte der neuesten Zeit 2).* Würzburg, 1962.

Alberigo, Giuseppe. ed. "L'Età di Roncalli," in *Cristianesimo nella storia 8* (1987), 1–217.

Algisi, Leone. *Johannes XIII.* Munich, 1960.

Andreotti, Giulio. *A Ogni Morte di Papa—I Papi che ho consociuto.* Milan, 1980.

Arendt, Hannah. *Menschen in finsteren Zeiten*, ed. Ursula Ludz. Munich—Zurich, 1989.

Bergerre, Max. *Ich erlebte vier Päpste. Ein Journalist erinnert sich*, Freiburg i. Br., 1979.

Capovilla, Loris. *Johannes XXIII. Papst des Konzils, der Einheit und des Friedens*. Nuremberg—Eichstätt, 1964.

——————————. *Ite, Missa Est*. Padua—Bergamo, 1983.

——————————. *Giovanni XXIII. Quindici Letture*. Rome, 1970.

Cousins, Norman. "The Improbable Triumvirate," in *Saturday Review*, Oct. 30, 1971.

Dorn, Luitpold A. *Johannes XXIII. Auf ihn berufen sich alle*. Graz-Vienna—Cologne, 1986.

Elliott, Lawrence. *Johannes XXIII. Das Leben eines großenPapstes*. Freiburg i. Br., 1974.

Fesquet, Henri. *Humor und Weisheit Johannes des Guten*. Frankfurt am Main, 1985.

Galli, Mario von; Moosbrugger, Bernhard. *Das Konzil und seine Folgen*. Lucerne—Frankfurt am Main, n.d.

Hales, Edward E. *Pope John and His Revolution*. London, 1965.

Hebblethwaite, Peter. *John XXIII, Pope of the Council*. London, 1984.

Helbling, Hanno. *Politik der Päpste. Das Vatican im Weltgeschehen 1948–1978*. Berlin—Frankfurt am Main—Vienna, 1979.

Johannes XX III. Das Leiden und Sterben des Konzils-Papstes. Ed. Katholische Nachrichten-Agentur. Bonn, 1963.

Johannes XXIII, Leben und Werke. Eine Dokumentation in Text und Bild. Ed. "Herder-Korrespondenz." Freiburg i. Br., 1963.

Kaufmann, Ludwig. *Damit wir morgen Christ sein können. Vorläufer im Glauben*. Freiburg i. Br., 1984.

Kaufmann, Ludwig; Klein, Nikolaus. *Johannes XXIII. Prophetie im Vermächtnis*. Fribourg—Brig, 1990.

Lazzarini, Andrea. *Johannes XIIII. Das Leben des neuen Papstes*. Freiburg i. Br., 1958.

Lenz-Medoc, Paulus. "Nuntius Angelo Giuseppe Roncalli. Erinnerungen," in *Hochland* 51 (1958/59), 497–507.

Lercaro, Giacomo Cardinal. *Giovanni XXIII. Linee per una ricercastorica*. Rome, 1965.

Mertens, Heinrich A., ed. *Ich bin Joseph euer Bruder. Chronik-Dokumente—Perspektiven zum Leben und Wirken Papst JohannesXXIII*. Recklinghausen, 1959.

Nikodim, Metropolitan of Leningrad and Novgorod. *Johannes III. Ein unbequemer Optimist*, ed. Robert Hotz. Zurich-Einsiedeln—Cologne, 1978.

Nürnberger, Helmuth. *Johannes XXIII. mit Selbstzeugnissen undBilddokumenten* (rowohlt monograph). Reinbek, 1985.

Pesch, Otto Hermann. *Das Zweite Vatikanische Konzil. Vorgeschichte-Verlauf—Ergebnisse—Nachgeschichte*.Würzburg, 1993.

Rahner, Karl. *Über die bleibende Bedeutung des Zweiten Vatikanischen Konzils* (Offprint n. 5 of the Katholische Akademie in Bavaria). Munich, 1979.

Rouquette, Robert. "Das Geheminis Roncalli," in *Dokumente. Zeitschrift für übernationale Zusammenarbeit* 19 (1963), 251–260.

Schneider, Theodor, ed. *Der verdrängte Aufbruch. Ein Konzils-Lesebuch*. Mainz, 1985.

Stehle, Hansjacob. *Die Ostpolitik des Vatikans 1917–1975*. Munich—Zurich, 1975.

Willam, Franz Michel. *Vom jungen Angelo Roncalli (1903–1907) zum Papst Johannes XXIII. (1958–1963)*. Innsbruck, 1967.

Zizola, Giancarlo. *L'Utopia di Papa Giovanni*. Assisi, 1973.

————————. *Quale Papa?* Rome, 1977.

INDEX